CHILD CARE
That
W O R K S

CHILD CARE That WORKS

How Families Can Share Their Lives with Child Care and Thrive

ANN MUSCARI AND
WENDA WARDELL MORRONE

DOUBLEDAY

New York · London · Toronto · Sydney · Auckland

PUBLISHED BY DOUBLEDAY
a division of Bantam Doubleday Dell Publishing Group, Inc.,
666 Fifth Avenue, New York, New York 10103

DOUBLEDAY and the portrayal of an anchor with a dolphin
are trademarks of Doubleday,
a division of Bantam Doubleday Dell Publishing Group, Inc.

Library of Congress Cataloging-in-Publication Data

Muscari, Ann.
Child care that works : how families can share their lives with
child care and thrive / Ann Muscari and Wenda Wardell Morrone. —
1st ed.
p.   cm.
Includes index.
ISBN 0-385-26391-0
ISBN 0-385-24728-1 (pbk.)
ISBN 0-385-26363-5 (Sp. Ed.)
1. Child care—United States.   2. Child development—United
States.   3. Children of working parents—United States.
I. Morrone, Wenda Wardell.   II. Title.
HQ778.7.U6M87   1989
362.7'12—dc19   88-38838
                                                    CIP

DESIGNED BY GUENET ABRAHAM

JUNE 1989
FIRST EDITION
BG

TO CHILDREN AND FAMILIES EVERYWHERE

CONTENTS

· · · · · · · · · · ·

Introduction   1

· · ·

PART ONE
GETTING STARTED

1. Exploring the Options   9
2. Learning What Your Limits Are   26
3. Understanding Your Child's Needs   41
4. The Successful Search   54

· · ·

PART TWO
DAY IN AND DAY OUT

5. Putting Your Best Foot Forward   73
6. The Ripple Effect of the Child Care Day   87
7. Rolling with the Punches: Problems with a Small *p*   98
8. Once-in-a-While Care   115

• • •

PART THREE
SHARING THE TOUGH STUFF OF CHILDHOOD

9.   Mastering the Universe: The First Two Years   133
10. Becoming Part of a Group: The Third and Fourth Year   146
11. Special Events: Celebrations and Character Builders   161
12. Problems with a Capital *P*   176

• • •

PART FOUR
SPOTLIGHT ON YOU

13. Nine to Five: How Child Care Affects Your Work   195
14. The Successful Rest-of-the-Week Parent   210
15. Your Supporting Cast   224
16. Living Cheerfully Ever After   238
     Index

AUTHOR'S NOTE

To avoid the constant and awkward
repetition of he/she and him/her, we have referred
to children as "she" and "her" in one chapter, "he"
and "him" in the next, and so on. We don't want
you
to think for a moment that some things will
happen
only with boys and others only with girls.
Everything may happen to everybody sooner or
later!

CHILD CARE
That
WORKS

INTRODUCTION

. . . .

Child care is such a hot topic today that most of us think we know a lot about it.

We're wrong.

Oh, we have a lot of information. We know how much child care is needed—we read that fifty-seven percent of mothers with children under six are in the work force now, for example. We know what's being done—the number of companies offering some form of child care assistance programs (thirty-three hundred), the unions with child care on their bargaining agenda (including the United Auto Workers, United Steel Workers, International Ladies Garment Workers Union). We've heard experts talk about possible effects on children in child care in such areas as language and aggression, as compared with children at home with their mothers. And we hear other experts talk about how hard it is to find child care.

What's missing from that comprehensive list?

The most important aspect of child care: day-to-day information on how parents and children can share their lives with child care *and thrive.*

For the twelve million families with children in some form of child care, statistics, expert comparisons, and nostalgic laments have little to do with real life. Success or failure with child care will be measured by the personal statistic of one or two children, and a discussion of whether or not their children would be better off with mother back home making lemonade and chocolate chip cookies is about as relevant as a debate on the value of fluoride in drinking water. Child care is just as certainly a fact of their lives.

And yet, even if they're presently using some form of it, most parents know startlingly little about when child care works well and why. "They don't want to know what quality care is," said one psychologist in the field, "because they're afraid they don't have it and they won't be able to find it."

Well, we do know what quality care is. We can tell you how to explore the possibilities, how to know when you've found it, and how to live with it once you have it. And because we know the answers, we can ask hard questions that many parents have avoided.

Do the best solutions vary from city to suburb to small town? From New York to New Mexico? From one neighborhood to the next? How much should a child's temperament dictate the child care you choose and when you begin it—and what if you can't afford the best choice? If your child is hyperactive, should you tell the child care center about his medication and run the risk of their refusing to accept him? Does your caregiver approve of your working—and if not, how will her opinion filter into her care? Do you know her birthday—and if you do and if you mark the day, how will *that* affect your child's care? How does child care change what you do with your child in the evenings and on weekends? How does it affect your workday?

Here, then, is the information you need to make child care work for you and your child—Monday through Friday, all year round. We'll discuss every aspect of child care, from how to find and recognize the best kind of care for your needs, to how to handle day-to-day questions like the sleeping problems of infants, whether toys at home should duplicate those at the center, or how to arrange child care so that brothers and sisters spend some time together every day.

We'll also talk about how parenting changes when you share your child's days with a caregiver. You can't check parental responsibilities at the door, whether it's the door to a child care center or to grandmother's house. Nor can you pretend that child care has no influence on a child's growth. The landmarks of childhood are permanently changed by the hours we share our children with child care. Toilet training is different (easier). Weaning a child from a friend the parent doesn't care for is different (harder). Everything we think we know about being an oldest or an only child is on its way to becoming obsolete.

If you are to stay in charge of your child's growth (and you must), you need to learn what your child's life is like each day; how to be sure that your parenting values are shared by your caregiver; and how to accept her, without guilt, as a creative partner in your parenting, one who can add the kind of excitement to your child's day that a good job can add to yours. You need to understand how to make child care providers feel they're doing a great job and how to help them do it; how to accept problems and how to solve them, as part of normal parenting rather than signs of a bad choice; how to instill in a child a sense of being a member of your unique family—with all its values, tastes, and idiosyncrasies —even when he or she spends most waking hours with others.

Obviously, what we're describing is a big and thoughtful part of a family's life. It seems scary at times because it's new to most parents—since few of you grew up in child care, you may often feel that you are pioneers, perhaps reluctant ones.

But no matter how isolated you may sometimes feel, you're far from alone. Mothers stay home in fewer than ten percent of today's families. In fact, women who don't work are joining the category of lottery winners or people on "Lifestyles of the Rich and Famous."

And the truth is, you are not so much breaking new ground as returning to a pattern as old as time. Perhaps you were taken care of only by your mother, but you can bet that your grandmother or great-grandmother cared for—and was cared for by—others. Everybody lived like the Waltons then, with a houseful of family members helping out.

To us, child care is the extended family of the future. We know you can manage this new life-style because millions of you are doing it now, with enthusiasm and imagination and practicality. What we want to do is share with you the trade secrets of doing it well.

PART ONE

GETTING STARTED

Each parent looking for child care has his or her own particular reasons. You may be five months pregnant, planning ahead. Perhaps your babysitter has walked out without warning and you need someone new by Monday. You're going back to work. Your mother, who has been taking care of the baby for the past six months, is going back to work. You or your spouse has a super job offer three states away. You've bought a house three neighborhoods away, which is too far a commute to your present child care center. You share custody, your daughter arrives in ten days, and it suddenly occurs to you that you can't spend every minute of the next three months with her. Your son, just turned two and a half, seems to be bored with his sitter.

Not only do you begin looking for child care for unique reasons, but the rest of your family agenda, from how many

. . . .

hours of care you need daily to how much you can afford to pay, is just as personal. That's why we're not going to tell you the best kind of child care for you: There's no way for us to know.

What we will tell you instead is what questions you need to ask—of each other and about your child, as well as about the different kinds of child care in your area—to make that choice for yourselves. Some you may already know, others you may not have thought about, still others may startle you. All will help you to put together a realistic picture of what you need, where to look for it, and how to recognize it when you find it.

We'll begin by describing the kinds of child care available and the advantages and possible pitfalls of each. Next we'll tell you how to put together your family needs package, based on everything from budget to where you live, and we'll discuss children's needs by age and temperament. Then comes the actual search: calling, looking, interviewing—and choosing the places and people with whom you will share the next few years of your child's life.

EXPLORING THE OPTIONS

. . . .

Child care includes your sister-in-law's baby-sitting three mornings a week, a nanny trained in nutrition and early childhood development, your next-door neighbor, a center like Kinder-Care, a cooperative nursery school—so many different varieties that it's tricky to describe the pluses and minuses of each accurately. However, it's possible to describe four basic types of child care: in-home care provided by a nanny, housekeeper, or au pair; a babysitter, whether at your home or hers; family day care; and center-based care.

Here, we discuss the basics of each system. We'll go into more detail about the kind of care nannies and sitters provide because it's hard for you to observe this kind of care in action. Since you can observe family day-care homes and centers, we'll tell you how to judge their setting in chapter four, when we discuss the interviewing process.

Nanny has become a catchword for any kind of in-home care

from mother's helper to babysitter, but the International Nanny Association is pressing for national nanny standards, including training in early childhood education, CPR, first aid, nutrition, and psychology. When we say nanny, we mean someone with that training, just as when we say housekeeper, we mean someone responsible for household duties as well as child care.

Otherwise, we'll use the more flexible term *babysitter*. A babysitter can be a relative or a neighbor. You may drive your child two blocks to your mother's each morning on your way to work, a neighbor may come to your house, a friend may take care of your child along with her own and one or two others. You may pay her by the hour (the most expensive) or by the day or by the week.

A *family day-care mother* also cares for a few children—up to five or six—but the relationship is a more formal one. She is registered through her state agency, which may mean her background has been checked, her fingerprints are on record, she has had a recent physical exam, and her house meets minimum safety standards.

Children in *center-based care* range from infants on up through school age. Ten years ago, care at such centers usually began at the age of two; now, in more and more centers, there is infant care starting at six weeks—though in this category as in every other, infant care is still the hardest to find. In many centers, care continues right up to school age, with preschool learning guided by trained teachers. It may even continue past school age—Kinder-Care, for example, offers after-school care for children up to age twelve, with vans delivering kids to school and picking them up afterward.

A center usually has a capacity for forty to a hundred children, though you may find as few as twenty or as many as two hundred twenty. The number of children (or license capacity) is determined by the state regulatory agency, as are the number of hours a center is allowed to operate (most centers are full-time, but a few are part-time). The regulatory agency also sets standards for safety, cleanliness, training of teachers, rest periods, food, and so on; a center must meet them all to earn a license—a stricter and more formal procedure than family day-care registration (which sometimes takes place by mail, without inspection).

Now, let's take a closer look at each kind of care.

LIVE-IN CARE

Nannies, housekeepers, and au pairs constitute the most expensive form of child care for one child. (They command a higher salary for more children, but not double or triple, so the economic comparison becomes more even if you have two kids and may even tilt in her favor if you have three or more.) Of course, rates vary widely throughout the country, but expect the cost of live-in care to be three or four times the cost of a child care center in your area, often in addition to room, board, and benefits.

Here's what you get for your money. While babysitters may not do household chores, for nannies and housekeepers, some chores come with the job. Doing the baby's laundry and preparing dinner are common. Family laundry and shopping are negotiable; cleaning is usually included in a housekeeper's job but not in a nanny's. If you can afford to have the cleaning done by someone other than the child care provider, we recommend it. Housekeepers who are passionate about cleaning get impatient with toddlers who follow behind them rumpling up the house. Conversely, if somebody is great with your child, you are not going to want to make an issue out of how often she should clean the refrigerator.

The number of household chores is not the only difference between housekeepers and nannies. Though a housekeeper may have had many similar jobs over the years, the chances are she settled into this career rather than planning for it. She's probably not trained for anything else (which she may or may not resent). In other words, she has had no courses in early childhood development, though she undoubtedly has the experience, patience, and common sense that comes from having raised children of her own. She'll probably be warm and loving with infants and toddlers, just as loving but less imaginative with children over three. Her ideas of what boys do and what girls do and of how and when to discipline will almost certainly be a generation behind your own. If the fit is good, a housekeeper may stay with you for many years.

Ideally, nannies have the professional qualifications we listed at the beginning of the chapter. A nanny sees raising young children as her chosen field; any one job is probably a stepping-stone toward a future goal, like opening a child care center of her own. Thus, on the one hand, her opinions and goals are current and her commitment very real; on the other hand, she will not be with you for long—two years at the most, say people at agencies.

For some young women, the length of their stay is part of the job definition. These are young women in their late teens or early twenties who come to you from another part of this country or from Europe. They're known as au pairs. The Europeans come chiefly from France, Sweden, England, and Germany; the Americans come from the Midwestern and mountain states. European or American, their range of motives is similar. They may be taking time off from college, postponing marriage (or looking for it), or simply eager to see another country or another part of their own country. Many, like longer-term nannies, see this as the first step of their careers. Their pay is similar too. If you pay under two hundred dollars weekly (plus room, board, with some form of driving privileges), count yourself lucky.

The chief difference between the European au pair and her American counterpart is language. We have heard of many, many European women whose English is not strong, and therefore limited vocabulary and tentative grammar are what your child will be exposed to for most of her waking hours. Experts debate whether or not this will affect your child's mastery of language, but many parents who have used au pairs feel that au pairs are generally not experienced enough for baby care anyway. They are at their best with young school-age children.

It's commonly believed that all parents would prefer live-in child care if they could afford it. Statisticians assume it—one Labor Department study used it as the premise for a child care comparison study. As a culture, we assume it. Television has just discovered family day care in "Day by Day," while housekeepers have been with us since "The Brady Bunch" and now star in "Charles in Charge," "Mr. Belvedere," and "Who's the Boss?"

There are clear advantages to live-in child care. As one mother said, "Even when she's sick, she's there." She's there not only when *she*'s sick, but when your child is sick, when you have to work late or go in early or travel . . . your coverage is theoretically complete.

But that's only part of the story. Although television shows overrepresent male housekeepers—there may be more on the three major networks than in the entire country—they dramatize at least one aspect of live-in care fairly. However the lines between family and caregiver are drawn initially, over time they begin to blur. You will learn your housekeeper's or nanny's tastes in rock music and celebrities, fill out her insurance forms, decorate her room, and worry about whether she should be allowed to entertain male guests there. You have a similar relationship with a babysitter, but if someone lives in, the relationship automatically intensifies. A babysitter is in *her* home at night. With in-home care, the housekeeper or nanny is in *yours*.

Not only is there a profound difference in privacy, but you may well find yourself in charge of finding her a social life, for the simple reason that unhappy people don't stay long. Thus, you'll become more knowledgeable than you ever thought possible about everything from the identities of other housekeepers or nannies in the area, to adult education courses, to reputable night spots.

Authority can also be a problem. Most of us are not comfortable with the concept of servants. You may have trouble maintaining a businesslike approach, listing what you want done, and holding your housekeeper to it without dropping into the style of asking for favors. The housekeeper or nanny may not be comfortable either. An older woman may feel her experience is much greater than your own.

Housekeepers and long-term nannies can be found through agencies, ads, or by word of mouth. This may be the hardest kind of care to find as well as the most expensive. According to the International Nanny Association, there are between seventy and ninety thousand requests for nannies each year, and only a small percentage of these can be filled by official nannies.

An agency has the advantage of offering you some protection against obvious dangers like theft or alcoholism or tuberculosis; it will also probably place its people "on the books"—that is, the relationship will be formalized with social security and the internal revenue service. Be warned, though, that many agencies will supply domestic help or babysitters and call them nannies.

When you interview people you've found through ads, it's up to you to check on the health and habits of your potential employee. Word of mouth—the friend of a housekeeper of a friend of yours—may mean that the woman you hire begins with a built-in social life. That's important. But it may also mean that your children will play with and be treated like the children in the other family. In other words, be careful whom you ask. With ads and word of mouth, your housekeeper or nanny may want to work off the books. (Aside from its illegality, off-the-books care isn't eligible for income tax credits.)

You will need help finding an au pair too. If you are looking overseas, you cannot research other countries very well from here. And finding a nanny from another part of this country is no cinch either. Since so much advance checking is necessary and the young women rarely stay more than a year, agencies can't really make money on this kind of placement. There are a few agencies that handle *only* this kind of care, but they generally stay in business for no more than two or three years. If you don't have access to a specialized agency, college babysitting services are a good starting place, as are ads in newspapers serving big Midwestern college towns.

BABYSITTERS

Nannies and housekeepers exist chiefly in the Northeast, California and, less commonly, in big cities in between. In most of the country, the person who cares for your child is better described as a babysitter.

Probably more parents turn to babysitters than to any other kind of care, though it's impossible to document the numbers. If the child care provider is a neighbor/mother/friend, probably neither parent nor provider troubles with the paperwork of social security or withholding forms. We're not making moral judgments about the legality of this, we're simply recognizing facts. The popular term for this is "off the books" child care.

Babysitting is special in several ways. It's undoubtedly the most affordable kind of care. The cost, like the numbers, can't be pinned down. Some grandparents may regard payment as an insult; for others the trade-off may be that you provide a new refrigerator when the old one breaks. You'll pay a neighbor more than the teenage babysitters in your area command but substantially less than a nanny. The feeling on both sides is more of doing one another a favor and less of money changing hands. It makes everybody feel good. The money your sister-in-law or friend or neighbor earns taking care of *your* baby may make it possible for her to stay home with her own. Your mother or mother-in-law is grateful for the chance to have a rare, real relationship with her grandchild.

There's a feeling of trust too. You assume that a neighbor, having chosen to live where you do, shares other values as well. The same goes for relatives and friends. Their definitions of everything from emergencies to discipline will be similar to yours; their goals for your child will be close to your own. You don't have to tell someone how you want things done—you don't even have to cope with the uncertain stages of building a relationship because it's there to begin with.

Finally, this is probably the most flexible kind of child care. Do you have a breakfast meeting? Grandma won't care if you drop him off an hour early. Is he sniffling? She'll take him anyway.

That's when it works.

Informal child care frequently stops working for the very reasons that made it so appealing to begin with. The first disadvantage is a very fundamental one: lack of reliability. The babysitter with whom you have a casual relationship casually backs out of it. When your aunt has a personal crisis in her life—whether it's a dentist appointment or a divorce—she doesn't have time to sit for you and she tells you so with no advance warning.

The second disadvantage is your lack of authority. True, you don't have to spell things out. But flip that over: You don't *get* to spell things out either. If your sister-in-law believes in toilet training at the age of one and you'd rather wait till your son is two and a half, how will you discuss that? Do you take it up with your husband first, since it's his sister? What if their mother gets involved? Right. You're not going to mention it. What if Grandma likes girls in frilly dresses and thinks they should play only with dolls and never splash through mud puddles? What if your neighbor disapproves of women working and treats your child with pitying kindness?

Few of these issues surface with babies, but they become increasingly apparent after children turn two. How often your child gets to play with other children (and who they are, and the character of the play), the kinds of toys available, the variety of activities— you'll find you have strong opinions on subjects you were deaf to a few months earlier. Negotiating each issue can be very difficult.

And, unfortunately, this kind of care can be as hard to get out of as it was easy to get into.

Then there's the other side: What if *you* abuse the relationship? Grandma may not like your being fifteen to thirty minutes late two or three nights a week. Perhaps your neighbor's son gets bronchitis easily and the colds he catches from your boy mean that the money you pay her is used up on doctor's bills. Maybe you let the weekly payment slip a day or two, just between friends. How will they bring up what troubles them? They'll probably just live with their sense of injustice.

Perhaps the greatest disadvantage of this kind of child care, though, is that it is vanishing. Ten years ago, it was estimated that fifty percent of all child care arrangements were of this informal kind; now the estimate has shrunk to between thirty and forty percent. Many grandmothers work; they've had time to establish careers; and they love being out of the house after all the years they spent as stay-at-home mothers themselves. They're neither willing nor able to sacrifice their new lives to fit your needs. Sisters-in-law and neighbors are asking for recommendations of good child care because they're working too.

FAMILY DAY CARE

Some babysitters care for several children in their home, still on a casual basis. But other women who do so put themselves on a business footing, the more formal care known as family day care. Ten years ago family day care was substantially cheaper than a child care center, but the gap is narrowing. Expect to pay between sixty and seventy-five percent of a center's rate; for hard-to-find infant care, the cost will be almost the same, sometimes even higher.

A family day-care mother cares for an average of five or six children (including her own). That's the limit most states set, but it's also what physical strength and sanity dictate. She may take infants as young as six weeks old (though in some states caring for an infant may limit the number of other children she can care for); she rarely cares for children (other than her own) over the ages of two and a half or three. Her fee occasionally includes meals, but most often children bring their own brown bag lunches. She can choose to accept a child with a cold or one recovering from chicken pox, whereas state regulations may forbid a center to do so. And although this is technically group care, many people consider a small self-contained group of children to be more flexible and low-key than a child care center.

There's no longer any nuance of a mutual favor about this relationship, and you are not a boss. Whether she has thought about it, a provider mother is an independent entrepreneur. She offers a service; you buy it.

A family day-care setting can be a warm, wonderful, extended family. The activities are likely to be similar to your own daily round: making beds, picking up, watching the garbage man, making lunch, taking naps, walking to the corner to mail a letter, maybe even taking a bus ride. Don't sell such activities short— some professionals speculate that these kinds of "real" tasks mean more to small children than child-oriented play. Cracking eggs into a bowl and spreading peanut butter may be heavy stuff to a toddler, particularly when she's part of a group of equally excited kids. Milestones that can be fraught with tension, like learning to drink from a cup or going up and down stairs or toilet training, happen almost before you or your child realize it. The lines of oldest children and only children blur into a gaggle of kids.

That's when it works.

When it doesn't work, one mother in the group regularly sends her son in with sniffles, which means your child struggles from one cold to the next all winter long. Or at the end of a ten-hour day, you find kids and caregiver alike whining with exhaustion. Or you discover that the changing table is also being used as the snack table. Or you learn the hard way—when your provider mother shuts up shop—that this is the form of child care with the least stability. (The turnover in family day-care homes is about one third every year, and some experts consider that a low estimate.)

Family day-care mothers can generally be divided into two distinct groups. The first is warm and loving but not necessarily stimulating: "They'll watch television a lot," said a partner in one agency. Like housekeepers, these are older women. Their own children are grown up, and either because they enjoyed children or because this is their only marketable skill, they turn to caring for children as a way of earning a living.

The second group is very different. It includes registered nurses, former teachers of the early grades, women in their forties and fifties who are simply tired of office work and want to come home, and women taking care of children so they can stay home with their own. For all these women, as for nannies, family day care is a rung on a career ladder. Many day-care mothers think they might move on from a day-care home to working for a child care center or running one of their own. They are apt to have conscious goals for the children in their care, as you yourself might. They provide a much more stimulating atmosphere than the women in the first group. And, as with parents, sometimes the atmosphere can be too stimulating, even pressured.

Family day-care mothers can be divided into two groups in a second way. Like housekeepers and nannies, some are off the books, and others are on—that is, registered.

There is an important difference, however. A housekeeper or nanny stays off the record largely to evade taxes; if you have found the right person, your child's care can be as good off the books as on. In a family day-care situation, though, that's not the case. While a day-care mother may want to avoid the bite of taxes and the accompanying mounds of paperwork, what matters to *you* is that she is also avoiding standards set up to protect you and your child—regulations, varying from state to state, mandate everything from fire extinguishers to courses in early childhood to kinds of toys. In a few states, a license requires little more than filling out a form and paying a fee, but many are more restrictive. Remember Jessica McClure in Texas in 1987? If her family day-care mother (who was also her aunt) had been licensed, the well into which she fell would have been sealed.

Licensed family day-care mothers are also becoming easier to find. In comparison to women operating off the books, who generally rely on cards posted in supermarkets, ads in local pennysavers, or word of mouth, registered family day-care mothers increasingly work through child care agencies. Some agencies have even begun to recruit and work with mother providers. Agencies offer advantages to both parent and day-care mother. Day-care mothers with the support of an agency generally stay in business longer because the agency plays the heavy: handling administrative details, collecting payment, and setting extra fees for lateness. An agency may assure you that it helps the parent as well, counseling you on what to look for in a family day-care home, for example. But the agency gets a commission for each client placed, often a part of each week's fee. Take their supposed objectivity with a grain of salt. An agency's waiting list is usually short because when working parents can't be placed immediately, they are forced to seek other care.

CENTER-BASED CARE

The largest groups of children and the most formal settings are found in center-based care. In a moment we'll discuss the several kinds of centers, but first let's describe a first impression of any center.

The most accurate picture that you can call up is probably the Sunday school classrooms of your childhood (and many churches that don't run their own preschools rent out their classrooms Monday to Friday for that purpose). The space for each group of children is much smaller than a school classroom and the children are in groups about the size of a Sunday school class—around ten, give or take a few. In centers designed and built for the purpose, the "classrooms" are delineated by cubbies serving as walls—private to a child's-eye view but open to adults. Space for infants is separate—usually the only closed door in a center, though the wall will have a big window—for health reasons, for parents to observe, and so that infants won't be bowled over by their elders. Since sunlight is important, infant areas will have lots of outdoor windows as well.

Children are grouped according to abilities—infants join toddlers as soon as they can walk. As they grow more skilled at walking, talking, and play, they move on to older groups. Within each group, there are enough activities for children to operate in groups of two- and three-year-olds. Each has at least one period of outdoor play each day and a rest period.

Generally, families provide the formula, baby food, and diapers for infants. Once a child moves on to the toddler group, she will have snacks in midmorning and afternoon as well as lunch; increasingly, centers provide hot breakfasts too.

Add up all that's happening and you come up with a fair amount of bustle, particularly if you're not used to the noise level of two- and three-year-olds. It will take a little time to sort out the underlying patterns, numbers of teachers, and how they interact with the children, and even then you'll need a guide. That's the center director. Since the women working with the children are called teachers, you probably assume that the center director occupies the slot of principal. Nothing so intimidating. She (rarely he) should be somebody who dresses like you, talks like you, laughs at the same things you do. For care in a center to work, you must bond with the director, trusting her implicitly to manage your child's care during the hours you are away.

Although first impressions of any centers have much in common, in fact there are several distinct kinds. The largest single kind is the church-sponsored centers—somewhere in the range of eighteen thousand throughout the country. (Estimates vary because in twelve states church-sponsored centers are not regulated.) There are centers that have been run by the same family for three generations. There are companies like Kinder-Care and LaPetite Academy and Discovery Centers that operate centers throughout the country. Some companies have centers at the workplace, called on-site child care, or, less accurately, corporate child care. A center can be in your neighborhood or near where you work or at your work place.

Now for the different types. *Church-sponsored nursery schools* and *neighborhood co-ops* are widespread, but they are intended to meet very specific needs. There may be an income ceiling, or families may have to be members of the sponsoring church or to volunteer time in the center. Frequently, the teachers and center director are working primarily because they are deeply committed to working with children and only secondarily for a salary. Going along with the commitment of the teachers, these centers generally have a strong point of view. Whether it is set by a board of church members or of parents, the philosophy of these centers is a strong part of what they offer. They have firm roots in their neighborhoods; center directors, teachers, and parents are probably also fellow church members, friends, and neighbors. The parent who enrolls her infant in a co-op may well be on the board in a year or two. If you share a church center's religious philosophy or a co-op's value system and feel strongly about raising your child within it, you'll trust this kind of child care in a way that is very hard to match; it may be the only kind that will really work for you. If your values are different from theirs, you may be uncomfortable there.

Then there are what are known as *Mom and Pop* centers. Mom and Pop seldom have more than a single center, which generally handles from twenty to forty children, though occasionally there are large centers, and here and there several units are owned by one person. Many such centers have been in business for generations: Daughter and eventually Granddaughter become the new Mom and Pop. What they do with kids hasn't changed much over the years and is apt to be the same highly personal version of what they did with their own kids. That may suit you down to the ground—many of the children in Mom and Pop centers, in fact, are children and grandchildren of their original charges. If you don't like how something is done, however, remember that Mom and Pop are probably not going to change.

The small size of these centers means that the directors know both parents and children well. Like church-sponsored or co-op centers, staff and parents may well be friends and neighbors outside child care hours. Often the people involved are running a center because they love children and have a personal vision of how children should be treated. That concern is reflected in the high quality of their nurturing, probably also in the meals they provide (though many small centers, like day-care mothers, require that children bring their own lunches). Fees range from slightly less than that of centers run as businesses to slightly more. And often they have the lowest rate of employee turnover—Mom and Pop are not going anywhere.

The small size that lends intimacy can be limiting, though, in the same way that not-for-profit centers are limited. Money has to go further. Insurance costs will be higher when only one center is involved. If Mom and Pop can't afford the van that larger centers have, that in turn makes it harder to arrange delivery, pickup of school-age children, and field trips. Playground equipment, craft materials, and programs may be scarcer. Since a single center probably can't afford a permanent staff of repairmen or painters, the director pays the same rates you do and the work is apt to be done at the same time: Monday to Friday, nine to five, while the children are underfoot.

The environment that most parents picture when the term *center* is used is one that is *run as a business*. These are the centers that look for what parents want and need and then organize to meet those needs. In some communities, that may mean hot lunches; in others, it may mean classes in computer skills and a second language. Some churches throughout the country lease space to groups operating this kind of center. There are vans for field trips; there are ample craft supplies; there are learning programs. Sometimes the rates are competitive with other centers and with family day care; sometimes the rates are higher.

A recent study has shown that parents who have never used child care prefer the idea of a national chain—it implies national standards of cleanliness and safety, more supervision of employees (and thus better protection from child abuse). On the other hand, parents worry that the directors may not be as warm or as responsive to their concerns. Many parents also feel that national chains have stricter rules about such things as clothes or food or admitting children with minor illnesses and are less flexible about late payments. All these concerns reflect a fear that a parent, as an individual, will get lost in the numbers of a national chain.

The centers getting the most publicity at the moment are those in the work place, or *on site*. The idea is that you take your baby to work with you, drop him off at the center, visit him for lunch (or even to nurse), and take him home with you.

On-site care is by no means a panacea. How many companies are large enough to provide the right balance of infants, two-, three-, and four-year-olds year after year? If a parent travels or is ill, who brings the child to the center? What if the baby is sick? What about traveling with an infant during rush hour? Finally and most importantly, at an on-site center, the company hires the center director—the woman who sets the tone for how children will be taught right and wrong, sharing, and honesty. How many parents want that choice made by their employer?

If a work force is homogeneous, though on-site centers can work well. Cigna, in Hartford, Connecticut, has a very successful child care center on their business "campus"—along with a shoe repair shop, a dry cleaner, and a post office. And national and political support for child care is growing literally from week to week. With the right tax incentives and rebates, on-site care may well become feasible for more employers to tackle: In the meantime, companies can support their employees' child care needs in many other ways that may actually help parents more. We'll describe them in Chapter 13.

In the end, whether a center is church-sponsored, run by Mom and Pop, or part of a chain makes little difference to you as a consumer. A center that's part of a national chain may educate you about standards of safety and cleanliness; if a church-sponsored or Mom and Pop center meets the same standards, fine. The owner of a Mom and Pop center may help you understand the importance of liking, respecting, and trusting the person in charge of how your child spends his days; if the director of a center that's part of a chain also seems like friend material, that's fine too. Since you need choose only one center, judge each solely on its own merits.

Each of these kinds of child care options offers different ways to meet the needs of you and your child. In the next chapters, we'll show you how to see clearly what your needs are. As you think about location and time and budget and your child's temperament, you may want to flip back occasionally to look at different kinds of care from your own personal perspective.

LEARNING WHAT YOUR LIMITS ARE

· ·

All parents seeking child care start with a personal list of things about their lives that can't be changed. Your combined take-home pay, for example, is on the list. Your job has certain requirements, whether you manage public relations for a school district and must attend school board meetings the first Tuesday of every month or whether you're a hairdresser who has to get in early enough to do some client's hair before *her* workday begins.

You may have other limitations that are just as inflexible though perhaps not as apparent. If you commute two hours a day, that long workday is on your list. If you have two or three children or you are a single parent, those special needs are on the list. Whether you want an active role in planning your child's care or want to choose someone experienced and leave most decisions in her hands, that preference is on your list.

All these examples fall into four categories of limitations: where you live, the kind of job you have, the way you want to be involved in child care, and, finally, what you can pay.

WHERE YOU LIVE

The kind of child care you need and what you can find are influenced in both obvious and subtle ways by where you live. If you work three blocks away from your home, obviously you require far different child care than if you work twenty miles away. When you're nearby, your caregiver needn't be able to drive, for example, because if necessary you can drop everything and race for the emergency room yourself. You can use your lunch hour to pick up the disposable diapers you ran out of and to schedule medical appointments. You can afford a caregiver who is less experienced and more dependent on you to make decisions (and almost certainly cheaper).

If you work twenty miles away, on the other hand, particularly if you rely on public transportation (whose efficiency is beyond your control), your choices are more complex. One possibility is to be out of the picture all day long. In that case, you opt for experienced and independent child care, whether that means hiring a very take-charge sitter (which may in turn mean that she is bossy rather than warm) or turning to a family day-care mother or a center. You are hiring someone who will take your kids skating or fishing or to repair a bicycle tire—someone who can handle the emergencies you can't get home for. One woman remembered with a shudder the afternoon her son fell from a climbing gym and broke his arm. She dropped everything and caught the first train, but the arm had been set and he was safely settled at home long before she could get there. Alas, he actually said, "You weren't here when I needed you. I don't need you anymore." Fortunately, she had a housekeeper who could drive and who kept her head so that her son's comment was the worst she had to deal with.

Whether she is sitter, day-care mother, or center director, when you work at a distance, you must feel confident that she can handle this kind of emergency.

You also need a good back-up system. If your housekeeper puts her hand through a window, who will drive *her* to the emergency room and take care of your kids? If your caregiver is ill, will a grandmother or a neighbor fill in for a day or two? When you work in the neighborhood, you can often make substitute arrangements on the spot; when you are twenty miles away, you must plan for trouble ahead of time.

Your child's age plays a role too. Up to the age of three, agencies find that parents prefer a caregiver or center nearer their workplace. The inconvenience of traveling with an infant or a toddler during rush hours is balanced by the comfort of being near at hand. When children are two years old or older, parents begin to see a value in child care close to home, so that children will get to know the children there, and share common experiences, ethics, and the territory of their own neighborhood.

The place you live also influences both the kind of child care you look for and—not at all the same thing—the kind you will find. This is true whether you are comparing neighborhood to neighborhood, suburb to city, or one part of the country to another. For example, studies show that throughout the country, a higher percentage of college-educated parents place their children in child care centers. Yet in Boston, New York City, Washington, D.C., and parts of the Los Angeles and San Francisco Bay Area, people in this demographic group turn in greater numbers to in-home care—sitters or nannies or housekeepers. Or two child care centers only a few miles apart may attract different styles of families—even though the centers may be owned by the same company. Why?

Two reasons. First, parents tend to seek the same kind of child care their friends and neighbors have, whether their neighborhood is a suburb or a network of friends scattered throughout a city.

Centers and agencies both find that parents most often come through friends' recommendations. Thus, whether your friends vouch for nannies or family day care or Miss McGinley's Country Day School, you too will see that choice in a favorable light. If you face the same long commute your co-workers do, you, like them, will be drawn to a center on the access road to the through-way—right on your way into the city. If you work in the neighborhood where you live, you'll turn instead to another center, near the first one, but on a side street, with both children and caregivers drawn from your neighborhood.

But parents also have to choose from what they can find, and the kinds of care vary greatly from one part of the country to another. Bankers who are perfectly satisfied with a child care center in Atlanta or Minneapolis or St. Louis or Dallas may move to New York and find that in-home care is the only kind available. College kids who take time out to become nannies for a year want to see the sights and sample the life-style of California or the East Coast; if you live in Chicago, you'll have more trouble arranging for this kind of care.

Again, why?

Often the underlying reason a kind of child care is not available is that it costs too much to provide. The rent for prime big city real estate would be over the moon. Or it may be staffing problems. The director of a part-time center on Long Island would have no trouble filling places if she switched to full-time care, but her teachers are interested in working only while their own children are in school. It may be that we're still trying to catch up to our needs. Part of the reason infant care is so universally hard to find may be that people in child care haven't had time to adapt to new mothers working.

Regulations are frequently a factor too. Massachusetts, for example, requires a ratio of one caregiver for every three infants (the national average is four to five). It's always difficult to argue with an ideal, but the practical result of this one is that infant group care in Massachusetts is all but impossible to find and too expensive for most of the parents who need it. Regulations may also drive many caregivers off the books. By specifying college-level courses in early childhood for workers, state regulations may shut out of the labor pool many of the women who have broad and rich life experience, which would be great for children, but little formal education. Reqirements for continuing staff training—again an admirable standard—may raise the cost of care beyond what many parents can afford to pay.

These geographical differences translate into real impact on people's lives. Two women stick in our minds. Both work as top executive secretaries, one in New York City, one in Atlanta; both have four-year-old sons. The New York woman has a long commute and a house too small for live-in care; her child care involves a precarious balance of a part-time preschool and her mother's help. When her mother can't help, she has even taken her son to the office—which means he misses his preschool and she must drive with him for an hour and a quarter each way in rush hour traffic. On one memorable day, copying her, he tucked notes of an important meeting into an envelope and, thinking it was the mail slot, put them down the chute to the incinerator. The woman in Atlanta pops her son into a child care center on her way to work and sometimes stops by for lunch. Both women would like to have a second child. Only one thinks she can manage it.

THE IMPACT OF YOUR JOB

The kind of jobs you and your spouse have is the second major influence on the kind of child care you need. There's an aspect of the life of two-job families that we feel is too seldom recognized: You are not always in control of your life. It may even be true that you aren't *often* in control of your life. The single greatest cause of failure with child care doesn't lie with the caregiver but with parents who try to get by with less care than they really need and then spend their days sliding for bases.

To get a realistic picture of the kind of child care you need to work at the level you need to, keep a diary—each of you—for a week. Note down what time you have breakfast, when you leave for work, what time you get home, what time you have dinner, what errands you do after work, how often unexpected tasks make you late. Are you rigidly required to be at your desk at a fixed time? How about your spouse? If neither of you can be flexible in the morning, you need child care either very close to home or very close to where you work so that you'll have one commute each morning instead of two. Most working parents are in this situation, by the way. In the evenings, conversely, people are much better able to move at their own pace.

Your job may have other, irregular time demands. Does one of you or do both of you work late frequently? travel a lot? have hours that change from week to week or month to month? Such requirements shape your choices in two ways. First, you must pick your child care and set up the schedule to suit the partner with the most stable job schedule and, second, the more special time requirements the two of you have, the more—and the more flexible—child care you must have.

Whatever your schedules are, write them down in detail. Two weeks would give an even better picture, but you probably don't have the time to spare. At the end of a week, you'll know what child care coverage you really need. This is what you must work with.

Besides time demands, a second aspect of your job may affect child care choices even more—and this one may surprise you—your job satisfaction.

We don't know what lies behind your pleasure, or lack of it, in working. The size of your paycheck? The people you work with? The work you do? It's likely, though, that your feelings about your job will influence your success or lack of it with child care.

Our observation is, first of all, that people who are unhappy with their work make poor choices in child care. If you are torn between work and home and some part of you is saying "You poor creature" when you drop your child off each morning, you'll have trouble seeing the advantages of any kind of child care. If you are stretched thin by tension at the office, you'll try to avoid thinking about child care as much as you can. You'll probably settle for the first affordable caregiver who doesn't foam at the mouth under a full moon.

Conversely, if you are content both with the idea of working and with your particular job, you'll look for—insist upon—an equally satisfying way for your child to spend *her* days.

Unhappiness on the job carries over on a daily basis as well. When people don't like their work, they try to close the door on it at the end of the day. That sets a bad example to a child—even a very young one—in ways far more important than you may realize. At the end of the day, when you pick up your child and ask, "What did you do today?" and the answer is a shrug or "Nothing," you feel shut out, don't you? A mother or father who doesn't share her/his day is doing the same thing. Your child needs you to pick her up and say, "Let me tell you about the people who came to our office today all the way from Salt Lake City. They installed a fire alarm system with a bell right outside my door. What happened to you?" By giving value to *your* day, you teach her to value hers.

Finally, unhappiness is draining. When parents work, a family's life is full and even over-full. Tension on the job will sop up energy you can't spare.

HOW INVOLVED DO YOU WANT TO BE?

A third major factor in the kind of child care you choose is how much you want to participate. Few parents today have a realistic idea of how to be a parent when they share their child's days with child care, perhaps because so few of the people choosing and using child care grew up with it. The head of a medical school recalls an intern who called the morning fall classes began, asking where to drop off her child. (The school didn't even offer child care.) Most day-care mothers have known parents who tried to drop their children off for the first time without leaving an emergency number or even a last name.

These parents are thinking of child care as a service, like a dry cleaner's. The point of a good dry cleaner is that, once you've found one, you can forget about that chore and get on with your life. But a caregiver is not an anonymous person in your life like your dry cleaner's. Child care will be a big, ongoing part of your life for the next few years. True, somebody else will be involved in some of the most important hours of your child's life, but that changes your role as parent—it doesn't eliminate it.

As we go along, we'll be discussing just how to parent hand-in-hand with your caregiver. You'll share concerns about your child, and you won't always agree on how to handle them. But over time, your caregiver—whether sitter, day-care mother, or center director—will play an important role in your lives, like a member of your extended family.

Beyond that fundamental emotional commitment, though, the amount parents become involved in child care varies markedly from one family to the next. Now—before you begin interviewing—is the time to decide how much and what kind of involvement is right for you because that choice will be reflected in your choice of care.

There is administrative involvement. If you have a sitter, you can (and sometimes must) control many daily choices, from food to friends—and many of those decisions, by the way, will be made over the phone during your workday. You won't have that much control with a day-care mother. In a center, administrative involvement would mean taking a role in decisions on such things as the age and background of caregivers, the kind of playground equipment, and planning meetings for parents. If that kind of involvement matters to you, look for a center with a parent supervisory board, whether run by an organization like a YWC/HA or a co-op center run by the parents themselves.

For other parents, it may be important that child care have certain attitudes toward religion or values. That is, although parents may not want to be personally involved in how a center is run, they may want its program to include specifics like grace at lunchtime and explanations of religious holidays. There are quality caregivers that provide this guidance and quality caregivers that don't. Whatever your feelings, be honest with yourselves and each other about this issue beforehand. Don't be like the father who chose an Episcopal preschool and then wondered, not too patiently, why his daughter asked so many questions about God.

Most parents are not interested in running a center, but they do want to know that the director is interested in their thoughts and ideas. Conversations at the end of the day, family nights where their children perform, Thanksgiving dinner for every family in the center—this is the kind of involvement that most parents are looking for.

STAYING WITHIN YOUR BUDGET

Last but, as no doubt you have already discovered, far from least is what you can afford to pay for child care. It's hard for parents to admit that cost has to be discussed. Everybody would much rather say that money doesn't matter, that you simply want what's best for your child.

But for all but a very few, that's just not the case. Child care will be the third- or fourth-largest expense in your yearly budget —after housing, food, and, depending on your income, taxes. You can't pretend not to care about an amount that large because you dare not let the cost spin out of control. You have to budget child care just like every other item; you have to live within that budget; and you need not feel guilty about that.

But—a most important but—living within a child care budget need not mean settling for less than your family needs. We stress this, because parents frequently make poor choices because they misunderstand budget priorities. See if you recognize yourself here.

The first choice is to stretch too far to afford the kind of child care you want. But you quickly come up against the fact of life we mentioned earlier: you don't have that much control over your life. There are unexpected doctor bills, car repairs; suddenly you need a new washing machine. Child care costs cannot consume an unmanageable portion of your budget.

Parents who have been burned by the first choice frequently make a second mistake: settling for a person or a center they don't really like or trust just because it's safely within their budget. In effect, they surrender and say, that's all we can do.

Let's be clear about this: We all have days when, in order to keep our lives going, our kids have to cope with illnesses or absences or sudden change. We wish they never had to, but it happens. But occasional emergencies are continents away from dropping a child off morning after morning at a place where you know she is bored and unhappy, even fearful. You won't be able to live with this. Don't even try.

Let us suggest a different approach. Begin by being as realistic about money as you were earlier about time: Which items in your budget are carved in stone? Which can you argue about? What does your spouse think you could do without (and vice versa)? It helps to make separate lists. The items mentioned by only one of you are the negotiable ones. Talk now, before you have fallen in love with a place, before you have even begun to interview. Then look at child care in a range of costs from a little below to a little above your target price. It helps to be able to picture how the kind of child care available changes as you go up and down the scale. What do you give up for less? Maybe too much. What do you get for more? Maybe less than you expected.

Be sure your comparisons are accurate. Are there penalty fees when parents are late picking up their children in the evenings? If you aren't being realistic about the hours you need, fines for being late can quickly make affordable care *un*affordable. A center that opens early and includes a hot breakfast and lunch may cost less in the end than one with fewer hours and no meals.

If you find that what you like is more than you can afford, don't settle for less. Instead, put together a combination of child care providers. Ask a relative to care for your child one or two days a week; then your budget will stretch to your ideal choice for the other three. If you don't live near any grandparents, a neighbor might babysit one or two days for a fee that enables you to afford something else the rest of the week. Ask your minister or priest or rabbi if someone in the congregation might welcome this kind of job. A couple in Washington, D.C., both of whom work full-time, and a single mother who works six hours a day have hired, together, a nanny that neither alone could afford.

You may think that combination child care sounds needlessly complicated. Actually, the reverse is true: when you set it up, you're also building in a back-up system for emergencies. If your neighbor gets sick, your child can doubtless go to the center for an extra day (for which you'll pay, of course); if your child gets sick and isn't allowed in the center, he can stay with grandma an extra day or two. And since the settings are already familiar, neither you nor your child will have the added stress of explanations or fears or tears.

FAMILIES WITH MORE THAN ONE CHILD

All working families have the requirements we've discussed so far. But some needs are special. When parents have two or more children, for example, every aspect of their lives, from getting the family out the door in the morning, to the hours they need child care, to its cost, becomes infinitely more complicated. There are two sets of appointments with the pediatrician and the dentist, two sets of clothes to shop for, two rounds of colds and flu and chicken pox—and two sets of emotional problems as well, from the feeding problems of little ones to the tragedies of broken friendships of older ones. Sometimes they happen at the same time. Family trips in the early years often become family circuses.

Your child care choices are more complicated too. One choice is to leave both kids with a day-care mother or sitter and assume that she is coping as well as you would if you were home. Here's the problem with that: Children's needs range so widely that a single caregiver has trouble meeting them. (More about this in Chapter 3.) The greater the difference in ages, of course, the greater this problem. But even the brief year or eighteen-month span that will mean little in ten years' time is an enormous gap between an infant and a toddler. The differing needs that exhaust mothers do the same for anybody else. The centers that offer field trips and wide-ranging programs that satisfy three-year-olds may not offer infant care. (Infant care is increasingly available at centers, but it's by no means universal.) The sitter who is a wonderful warm presence with an infant may not have the language skills or patience needed to deal with the endless questions and stampeding energy of a three-year-old. Whether they're aware of it or not, sitters and day-care mothers tend to specialize in the ages they like best—usually babies.

When you're caught in this bind, the unspoken emotional cost to you can be very high. If you know that your older child is spending Monday through Friday in front of a television set, you'll feel compelled to fill evenings and weekends with high-compression parenting—trips to the library, gymnastics lessons, simple science experiments, number and letter games.

In some parts of the country, the combination child care we described earlier is the best solution. Perhaps the infant spends the day with a sitter while the three-year-old is at a center, or the toddler is at a center while the older child goes home after school to a neighbor.

There can be a serious problem with such arrangements, however. As the children's books say—what's wrong with this picture? Your children may not spend any time with one another. Siblings are born, but sibling *relationships* must be forged by day after day of pulling the pots out of kitchen cupboards and turning the shelves into bunk beds, feeding bread crusts to ducks, fighting over Monopoly. If you want brother and sister to *understand* that they are brother and sister, your child care arrangements must reflect that wish.

It isn't always easy. Perhaps both children can spend the morning with a day-care mother or housekeeper who will walk the three-year-old to a center or nursery school for the afternoon. If you can find a day-care mother close enough, the older child can join the younger one there after school. Increasingly, child care centers care for a broad age range—Kinder-Care, for example, cares for six-week-old infants on up through age twelve. The advantages this provides for both you and your children are obvious. They can grow up with a sense of themselves as siblings—and you can do one schedule instead of two or three.

One problem with even the best arrangements, of course, is the cost. If your children are with a day-care mother who cares for your infant full-time while the older child goes part-time to a center, you may end up paying her for full-time care of both children—the part-time care of your child, after all, keeps her from caring for another child full-time. If she's registered with an agency, frequently the agency will absorb a small price break in its fee, allowing the day-care mother to make the same amount. Centers may negotiate a reduction for part-time care and reduce their rates fifteen to twenty percent for second and third children.

With three or more children, the weekly cost of child care becomes formidable. The most feasible care would be someone who lives in, a kind of care unavailable in most parts of the country, even if she could meet the needs of children of three different ages. Many parents with three or more children are making trade-offs they'd rather not make, whether a parent gives up a job to be home, or the youngest is in child care while the older ones fend for themselves. And yet many others, perhaps because they're aware that this expensive and hectic phase is also a short-lived one, seem to be sailing through it.

THE SINGLE PARENT

Another special situation—also a common one—is the family headed by a single parent, almost always the mother. Single parents would probably agree on the two difficulties they all share. The first is not enough money! Child care costs don't come down just because there is only one salary to cover them. Neither do the costs of children's shoes or groceries.

The second is not enough time. One parent must cover ground that is more than enough for two. One parent must do all the dropping off and all the picking up. Because one parent is in sole charge, minor inconveniences like working late, shopping, and errands quickly escalate into crises.

Shortages of money and time inevitably have their effect on your choice of child care. You're caught in the double bind of needing more care yet not being able to pay top dollar for it. You really need the kind of arrangement provided by a sitter or, more formally, a day-care mother. Because her registration doesn't cover hours of care as a center's does, she can be flexible about lateness as a center cannot. And while centers tend to discourage the use of their teachers as sitters after hours, a day-care mother may be willing to sit for you in the evenings or on weekends to give you some of the privacy every parent occasionally needs while giving your child the reassurance of a familiar face.

Single parents also have to be honest about their need for support from family and friends. We think of one young mother, a nurse who had a challenging, well-paying job on a heart-surgery team in Texas, working in a hospital that provided on-site child care. That sounds ideal, doesn't it? Yet within six months of her daughter's birth she had moved back to her hometown in Iowa. She needed the added cushion of support that only her family could provide. We all need that support, as we'll discuss further in Chapter 15. But single parents learn the lesson first and get few chances to forget it.

Your jobs, where you live, the size and shape of your family, the involvement you want with child care, what you can pay—the picture is almost complete. The missing piece is what your child is like and what he or she needs. And that's the subject of the next chapter.

C H A P T E R   T H R E E

UNDERSTANDING YOUR
CHILD'S NEEDS

· ·

There are perhaps a half dozen children in the room, all roughly a year old. One girl, walking with the ease of an old hand, dashes in and among the cribs as though they were part of a climbing gym. Under one crib sits a boy with a jack-in-the-box, solemnly winding the knob till the clown pops out, pushing him down till the box clicks down, winding the knob again. Across the room a teetery brand-new walker pulls herself from crib leg to crib leg, tries to bridge the gap between with two quick steps and smacks face-first to the carpet, too inexperienced to put up her hands to protect herself. In the middle of the room two children sit while one reads *Pat the Bunny* to the other—no words are comprehensible, but her voice lilts up for questions and sometimes comes down with great emphasis (and an accompanying scowl). Now and then she reaches out for her companion's hand for him to pat and touch and rub. He waits peacefully, submitting his hand when required, to all intents and purposes unaware of his role.

All different. All normal.

Your child's needs and tastes and style are every bit as complicated and fascinating as your own. Some relate to age: Six-month-olds have learning tasks and needs in common, as do three-year-olds. Others relate to the particular, unique little person that he is and will be, no matter what his age. Some needs influence the way he will react initially to child care—any kind of care—and others will shape the way he responds once he has settled into a routine.

As in setting a budget, you will probably begin with the thought that only the ideal is good enough for your child, never mind the strains it might put on your jobs, your pocketbook, your lives. That's admirable and understandable, but it's not quite right. Ideal care is what works best for your child—and also fits in with your budget, your job, and the needs of you and your spouse. If the two of you sacrifice too much to child care, no matter how fine it is, it's not ideal. Your satisfaction with your job and your pleasure in each other as partners and parents also provide irreplaceable things for your child, after all.

We begin with this statement because we want you to think about the information that follows from the right perspective. Of course, children have significant needs relating to age and health and temperament, and of course these needs play an important role both in your choice of child care and in how you and your caregiver work with your child. But your child's needs do not singlehandedly *dictate* your choice.

YOUR CHILD'S TEMPERAMENT

Let's talk first of all about the kind of person your child is, whatever his age. Talkative or still, restless or serene, easily distracted or able to concentrate for long moments—all are signs of a child's temperament—not intelligence but personality. Studies have shown that parents have a good picture of their infant's style within days of birth—which is handy, since studies show further that an infant's temperament seems to continue into adulthood. The one-year-old who makes everybody in the house miserable for a week before he takes off and walks will more than likely turn every major learning experience in his life into high drama, from making friends to learning to ice-skate to getting married. If your baby is a watcher whose quiet reactions take time for you to figure out, she'll require just as much effort and thought from everyone who deals with her in the years to come. That's why we need to take our child's style into account in choosing his or her child care setting.

Children generally can be described in one of three ways—the *difficult* child, the *easy* child, and the vast majority of children who are a *mixture* of both. Difficult children are easy to spot. They fuss, like the example above. They're not very flexible—whether it is with regard to what they eat (and when, and in what high chair, and with what spoon, and with what teddy they share the chair), or when and how much they sleep, or the clothes they wear, or the order in which they put them on. You name it, and difficult children have one special way they want to do it. Period. They change reluctantly. They are intense in their reactions and in their play. Theirs is a black-and-white world.

Easy children are pretty much the opposite. Their reactions can be so low-key that you may have to watch carefully to see when they are unhappy. They accept whatever food is offered. Their patterns may not be strongly ingrained. They sleep seven hours one night and ten the next, nap heavily one day and forget to do so the next, eat heartily Tuesday and nibble on Wednesday. They may not demand as much involvement from you. You can plop an easy child on the living room floor and she will still be playing quietly when you go back half an hour later. (The difficult child would have all the books and sofa cushions on the floor and be tackling the piano.)

Most children fall somewhere in between. Some may have all the traits of the difficult child but to a less extreme degree; others are as accepting as the easy child but livelier. Still other children mix up the traits—rigid in some areas, easygoing in others. This latter group can be maddeningly hard to understand. A gentle child, for example, can also be an intense one. Somehow we're more geared to accept the child who expresses his dislike of spaghetti by heaving his plate to the floor than the one who pushes it slowly away, and then, when you coax, accepts a mouthful only to let it drool back out again.

What happens to each of these children when he or she hits the world? Studies have tracked kids, some for over twenty years. You might think it would be easy to predict what kind of treatment makes a child with a particular temperament flourish and what cramps her style, and sometimes it is. The difficult child, for example, intense himself, tends to provoke intense responses. Some parents are overwhelmed by his energy, while others delight in it. Few are neutral. The easygoing child may disappoint some parents, while others may take a quiet pleasure in her gentle cues. A child who is a mix of qualities may be misread frequently—the gentle intensity described above may be interpreted as stubbornness. You may keep on struggling to convince a gentle, easygoing child and be frustrated—and furious—when you don't succeed, whereas you would quickly learn to avoid unnecessary confrontations with a screamer and would probably be less apt to blame him for the likes and dislikes he so obviously can't control.

There are also surprises. When easygoing children interact with people other than their own families, they frequently have temperament-linked problems that their parents have never come up against. Because they aren't restless, because they aren't obnoxious when they're bored, their parents haven't often had to distract them—which may mean that they haven't had a broad range of experiences or much practice in adapting to new situations. Parents may not even realize that their children have trouble adapting because they have never had to do it. Thus, these shy children hang back in their first experience with other children or with school. By the time they are ready to stop watching and participate, groups are set and adults' impressions are formed. And changing the status quo may be difficult. Because quiet children have subtle cues, their overtures may be overlooked. Because they are not fighters, they may shrug and withdraw.

Bear these findings in mind as you interview sitters and look at child care settings, remembering that there are no automatic rights and wrongs. If you have a quiet child, for example, do you assume that a sitter will be the most responsive to his gentle cues and will have the most time for one-on-one attention? Or do you wonder that if your baby doesn't sit up and scream for attention, the sitter may feel free to spend her day watching the soaps? Do you assume that the quiet child will be overlooked in the hubbub of a center? Or do you consider that a center has so much more for a watcher to watch that she won't ever be bored? Do you think a restless child will be too exhausting for one person to care for all day? Or do you conclude that he may need the tolerance and understanding that comes from a close, long-term relationship with a single caregiver?

HEALTH PROBLEMS

His style is part of your child's individuality. His health is another. How do health problems affect child care arrangements?

Having severe allergies is probably the one common health problem that makes group care a question mark for some children. If a center requires that children bring their own lunches, you can try to work around food allergies—but you have no guarantee that she won't trade her safe sandwiches for Twinkies. Dust, the dander from the pets of other children that inevitably sticks to their clothes and then rubs off on the allergic child's—a child may be able to cope with a few problems but not a long list. Don't forget, too, that a child who is using her resistance to cope with allergies may be more vulnerable to other illnesses such as colds. If allergies do seem to make group care difficult, though, that will be the parents' decision, not the day-care mother's or the center director's.

Some children have emotional problems—violent temper tantrums, depression, autism, a history of physical or emotional abuse. In such a case, you'll want the advice of your pediatrician and/or a psychologist to help you determine which kind of care is the most reasonable solution.

Few family day-care mothers or center employees can sign for hearing-impaired children. Similarly, they have neither the training nor the insurance to handle breathing machines or heart monitors. Special children deserve special environments, where their interests can best be served.

PHYSICAL AND EMOTIONAL MILESTONES

Besides her own personal package of style and health, your child has many moods and learning tasks in common with every child her age. That's been so since she was a newborn and you were counting the days till she smiled or slept through the night, and it will be true in the years to come.

You're familiar with some of the milestones, of course. First teeth arrive at about six months old. Babies walk when they are roughly a year old, begin to pick up words even before then, and are forming simple sentences when they are about eighteen months.

These achievements are easy to spot and recognize. The milestones of mental and emotional mastery are every bit as predictable to experts. If you're not an expert, though, some of the stages can be baffling. In the first few months of an infant's life, for example, it's important for parent and child to fall in love, solidly and forever. ("Stabilizing the attachment" is the clinical description of it; another term is "bonding.") Parents worry that returning to work too early will interfere with that process, say pediatricians and psychologists, but they tend to talk instead about lack of time and finding good child care—it seems to be hard to admit to a reluctance to leave a baby when you didn't even know him a few weeks ago.

Stranger anxiety can be puzzling too. Up until about eight months, babies respond readily to a caregiver. Parents, grandparents, babysitters, center teachers—she may have special smiles for you, but she'll gurgle and coo with anybody. Sometime between six and eight months, though, a baby learns the meaning of the word *stranger,* and she invests that word with the dread terror of the heroine of a gothic novel. Her fear continues roughly through the age of eighteen months, when her confidence grows to the point of wanting to explore the outside world.

There are other tasks that children master at roughly the same ages. In the first two to two-and-a-half years, the foundations for language are laid. Two-year-olds spend their time discovering, repeating, and testing their environment and all the people in it. Their behavior is apt to be uneven—making great strides in some areas and none at all in others. Three- and four-year-olds are always in motion, beginning to follow directions and to relate to other children.

HOW YOUR CHILD'S PATTERNS SHAPE YOUR PARENTING

What do these patterns mean to you? First, you try to protect them as much as you can. Try to preserve the initial attachment process by taking three months' parental leave. You and your child will find work and child care easier if you do.

Work around stranger anxiety too. If your baby is in some form of child care before eight months, she will take it for granted (always allowing for differences in temperament). In the period between six to eight months and eighteen months, she will be much more fearful and/or resentful of any kind of care. If she is settled in one kind of child care by six months, she may find it difficult to switch to another setting—again, that means going from the familiar to the strange.

When you have a choice, then, obviously you'll avoid big changes between eight and eighteen months. If she's not in child care when she's eight months old, you may want to wait till she's roughly a year and a half. And you'll try to avoid changing from one kind of child care to another. This means, by the way, that an au pair or a nanny from the Midwest is a poor choice for your baby's first caregiver. Why? Because she signs on for only a year. Maybe you could convince her to stay on, but then again maybe you couldn't.

The fact of the matter is, though, that parents don't always have a choice about returning to work or beginning child care or changing from one kind to another. You may find that your family needs two incomes, or you or your spouse may be transferred. A child care arrangement may collapse—your day-care mother decides to retire, your nanny leaves after her year is up, the teacher at the center takes an office job. What then?

Because so many things can happen, we recommend that you take your infant to the homes of others (grandparents, friends) frequently in the first months of her life even if you still have leave, even if your babysitter or grandmother or other in-home care is working out just fine. Then if you do return to work at a time that's less than ideal for one or the other of you, the adjustment will be a little easier.

If you haven't done that, use what you know about your baby's fears to help her adapt to her new setting. You will want to introduce whichever care you choose more slowly after eight months to allow your child an adjustment period. That may mean working on a part-time basis for a few days, even weeks, longer than you had planned, and spending the hours, instead, home with the caregiver or visiting at the center. It may be that all you can do is accept the fact that life is going to be stressful for her for a while, and try to be warm and patient when she clings and whines and wails when you leave. It doesn't mean you have an unpleasant child. It means she's having a rough time at the moment.

Let us hasten to reassure you. Before and after the age of stranger anxiety (and often during this period too), many children seem to handle a change in child care much more readily than their parents do. If a child is moving from any other kind of child care, she has already been exposed to changes and begun to accept that as a part of life. If she was at a center, she knew at least four adults— the director, the cook, her teacher, and her part-time teacher. She saw other teachers on the playground, and she saw the mothers of other children. She's an old hand. You'll notice this when you interview at any kind of group care. A child is much more apt to run up to you and say, "Whose mommy are you?" than to shy away from you.

The learning tasks of a certain age—like language in the first two years and becoming part of a group at age three and four— can help to guide your choice of caregiver and care. You can't expect a caregiver to be an expert on a given age, but you can see if she has the qualities that are needed—lots of conversation for infants and toddlers, lots of patience for two-year-olds. Because so much of what three- and four-year-olds do needs to be done with other children, parents almost always turn to some form of group care by this age. (You can see the qualities that make a caregiver successful with these age groups by watching groups in action, so we'll talk more about them when we discuss interviewing, page 55.)

TO PUSH OR NOT TO PUSH

One last thing that applies to all of a child's learning tasks. A child will learn to handle each task best not by being pushed but by reaching the age at which she's ready to learn it, whether it's talking, learning to recognize letters and numbers, understanding what more than one of something is ("more two," said one frustrated toddler), learning how to stand up for what she wants and how to share. She will learn them with confidence and grace *at the proper time.*

We stress this because in the opinion of many people who spend a lot of time with children (including us), a growing number of parents seem to have lost faith in the ability of their children to grow, on their own, with confidence and grace and joy. Instead, they are signing up their three-year-olds for violin and tennis classes. They are buying phonelike electronic marvels to press against the uterus, supposedly to teach rhythm to the unborn infant. They (parents, not children) are mesmerized by flash cards. A nanny with a second language is viewed as a prize (you hope she'll make your kids bilingual). A center's ad may promise that three-year-olds will learn computer skills.

The pressure on children has become so widespread that it even has names—hothousing, superbaby syndrome. One of the wisest men ever to work with children, David Elkind, has gone to the length of writing a book deploring this pressure *(Miseducation: Preschoolers at Risk).*

Hothousing, or miseducation, or pushing, is a matter of grave concern. Look at the probable effects on the child. Artificial learning in infants and toddlers happens only through rote memorization rather than the Eureka! of discovery. A child continually pressured to learn this way also learns that her parents value memorization over discovery and ideas; she will eventually absorb that value as her own. Then too, because she is praised for artificial achievements, she'll assume that her parents value her for these achievements rather than herself.

The pressure to learn before she's ready means that, even if she succeeds, a child feels fearful and anxious instead of joyous and triumphant. When she fails, she blames not her misguided parents but herself. If she's pushed too far physically—by concentrating on a single activity like tennis or gymnastics or swimming instead of the normal whirligig day of a preschooler, she will be straining her growing bones, muscles, tendons, ligaments in one direction only, probably beyond their limits.

The immediate signs of hothousing are those of any stress: sleeping and eating problems, stomachaches, headaches. In the long term, the groundwork is being laid for adults who will be anxious, fearful, self-blaming, who will parrot back concepts instead of discovering their own, who may develop early arthritis or tendonitis or "green-stick" fractures. Privileged children indeed!

What never has the chance to happen is also worth noting. That is, when an infant/toddler/preschooler is forced to fill her time with flash cards and violin lessons, she can't be about the business appropriate to her age. For an infant, that may mean watching her waggling fingers for minutes on end. For an eighteen-month-old it may mean playing endless games with singsong syllables that sound meaningless to nearby adults. For a four-year-old it may mean using bathroom language at inappropriate times and then laughing at her daring. It's called play, and *that*—not adult-directed pseudo-learning—is the work of children.

Whatever her age, a child going about her business should show curiosity, explore, set her own goals (sometimes indecipherable to an adult), and finally, she should show a mastery as joyous and immediate as the bulb suddenly lighting up over a cartoon character's head. The day a four-year-old learns to skip, she should be skipping triumphantly till she topples over in delicious exhaustion.

One particular task of three- and four-year-olds is so essential that we'll discuss it at greater length in Chapter 10—the matter of becoming part of a group and making friends. These are the years when a child should be making a new best friend almost on a weekly basis, squabbling and making up day in and day out. We mention it here because it's a task easily sacrificed when a child is forced into formal learning too soon. She has no time. Her relationships with other children get pushed down the priority list, and she learns not to value friendship. Worse still, when groups begin to form, she hasn't learned the skills to join them easily and confidently. Since she is also learning an anxious and self-blaming mindset, she may assume that the problem is inborn, that she isn't worthy of friendship.

Why do parents increasingly feel the need to push their infants and toddlers? Guilt is a part of it. If I can't be with my kid, reasons the parent, I'll see that her care is even better than I could provide.

And why is it so easy to assume that forced learning skills are the best definition of "best"? As a society, we're goal-oriented. Why should parents of young children suddenly become immune? The mastery of a skill like how to use a computer is a goal, and such goals convince us that we must be getting our money's worth. Besides, such skills are easy to see and understand, unlike the slow unfolding of independence and creativity and the ability to sense another child's needs. Finally, learning skills are convenient buzzwords. If you murmur "computer skills" and "second language" at a cocktail party, everybody knows they're supposed to translate that as "quality." This is particularly true if the other parents present are using the same buzzwords. It's hard to defend to these parents the value of your child comforting another, smaller child who has had a toileting accident. For all these reasons, busy parents all too frequently think of learning skills as a convenient synonym for quality in child care.

The important thing to bear in mind as a defense against outside pressure is that children *will learn,* in the fullness of time. And there won't be a space on your daughter's college applications to mention the fact that she took preschool computer classes. *Child care is not the place for formal teaching.* When you look at child care settings, don't be bewitched by the sight of children being drilled in aerobics or a second language or tennis lessons. Instead, look for children who are playing in a half-dozen different ways. You may not understand the purpose of their play, but you should be able to judge the emotional state of the kids: intent but not anxious, curious rather than fearful. These are signs of children ready to learn, children who will be joyous rather than relieved when they triumph.

THE SUCCESSFUL SEARCH

· ·

You now have a working picture of possible kinds of care, of your child's needs, and of the family's needs. Next comes the crunch—actually choosing the child care setting that best fits your family's needs. There are several steps to the process. First, obviously, you have to find potential caregivers to interview. Next you need to prepare for the interview, to clarify what you are looking for so you won't waste your time. Then there is the interview itself and, finally, assessing what you have learned and making your decision.

SOURCES FOR CAREGIVERS

People search for child care in one of three ways—word of mouth, advertising, and agencies. *Word of mouth:* a co-worker gives you the name of her family day-care mother; your sister has used a terrific center; there's a conversation after church; some of your neighbors use a Montessori school two blocks away. Most people have an unconscious desire to use the same kind of care that friends, neighbors and co-workers do. There's a certain trust involved. These are the people you are most comfortable with; it stands to reason that you want your child raised similarly to theirs. Most caregivers agree that word of mouth is their biggest source of clients.

It has its drawbacks, however. Often people fail to check out word-of-mouth sources as rigorously as they would unknown ones —as though a businesslike thoroughness somehow implied mistrust of neighbor or relative. And what if, in the end, you choose a center over the Montessori school that is the neighborhood favorite? Your neighbors might wonder why you asked for advice only to ignore it.

Advertising can be in the Yellow Pages, on the bulletin board in the grocery store, in your local newspaper or pennysaver, or through direct mail. You may place ads asking people to call you and potential caregivers may place them describing their services. If friends and neighbors have no recommendations, if all their choices have long waiting lists, or if you want a more complete picture of what's out there, ads are your next option. On the one hand, it's scary to approach a stranger about something as serious as the care of your child. (It's a legitimate concern, too, because an ad tells you only of availability. There is no guarantee and no guidance. In many states, a caregiver may *advertise,* even though she doesn't meet state standards, has no license, and cannot legally *operate.)* On the other hand, you may think you'll be able to be more objective with the strangers you find through an ad, better able to ask tough questions and state tough demands. That's true up to a point, but as one mother pointed out, a family day-care mother or center director or nanny is a stranger only for the first few minutes. You may still feel awkward asking if she has had an X ray to check for tuberculosis within the past year or ending an interview without making a decision.

Through advertising, you also find a third source for child care: *child care agencies.* There are agencies that specialize in one kind of care—day-care mothers or sitters, for example. If you already know what kind of care you want, a special agency will save you time.

Although an agency must have a license, usually issued by a city or state consumer affairs department, sitters need not meet the same health or fitness standards as family day-care mothers or center employees. And the woman an agency calls "nanny" may have no more training than what we define as "sitter." Always check and keep checking.

There are also about six hundred resource and referral agencies nationwide—not nearly enough, but you should be able to find one in most metropolitan areas. (If you don't find a listing in the Yellow Pages, the National Association of Child Care Resource and Referral Agencies, Rochester, Minnesota, 507-287-2020, can give you some names in your area.) A good R & R will walk you through much of the information we've discussed. It will make recommendations in any and all areas of child care without trying to make your choice for you. It may even help you get started and act as a go-between in case of misunderstandings. *Drawbacks:* If an R & R is operated by a public agency, it may not list the private centers in your area, making a choice for you (sometimes without telling you) that you might prefer to make for yourself. And of course, you pay for an agency's help, sometimes with a higher weekly fee, sometimes with a flat fee upfront. For example, of a seventy-five-dollar weekly fee for a day-care mother, fifty-five dollars may go to the mother and twenty to the agency.

WHAT PARENTS LOOK FOR (AND OVERLOOK)

However you compile your list of names, once you have several of them, you move on to the next step—preparing for the interview or visit.

All parents have certain common goals for child care—basically, a loving person. If the care will be outside their home, they are concerned as well with safety and cleanliness. But, although they're seeking the same information, parents go about it very differently, beginning with the initial phone call. And the differences show caregivers what their unspoken—and perhaps unconscious—concerns are.

When parents use that first call to ask questions that most parents save for an interview, they are telegraphing the fact that cost is their overriding concern. They don't want to explore what they can't afford. Three other attitudes show up quickly in the interview. To one group of parents, location is everything. This may reflect a concern with safety—some parents won't choose a center beside a major roadway, no matter how convenient. It may be a matter of time—a parent with a complicated commute must have a center that keeps it as simple as possible. And it may be a matter of neighborhood—I want my child where I live.

A second group of parents wants to be able to picture the child's day. How big or how small does the center seem, what room would my child be in, who would the other children be, who would his teacher be. These are people who need to touch and feel and see in order to make their decision. Without being aware of it, they're seeking an atmosphere similar to the one they create around them in life. If you like lots of talk and people, you'll like the bustle of a center or a family day-care home and may find in-home care boring (unless the sitter is a one-woman band). If you like a quiet, contemplative atmosphere, the reverse may be true. If you are active and athletic, the playground equipment and games will draw your attention. This is unfair only if you're unaware of what you're doing. Then you're apt to think of your opinions as judgments of good and bad rather than your taste versus someone else's. That in turn may lead you to overlook the taste of another important person—your child.

A third group of parents is very knowledgeable about the current literature. They'll ask a caregiver's opinion of Piaget or how the learning methods compare to those of Montessori. Warmth or lack of it, convenience or lack of it, playground equipment or lack of it won't enter into their decision, but their ability to identify with the director will.

As you can see, all have their strengths and their blind spots. If you're lucky, you can be drawn to a child care setting that satisfies your personal agenda and find that the basics are taken care of as well. Or a good nanny or day-care mother or center director may point out what you haven't asked. But it's best to go into an interview with all perspectives in mind. You want to avoid making a choice based on your first attraction and then discovering once you have begun the routine that other things matter more.

There is a final blind spot that nearly all parents share. Parents limit themselves to looking at *child care*—safety, cleanliness, location, and so on. But, just as important, you are looking for *support for yourself.* You are heading into uncharted waters, parenting in ways for which there are few role models. In order to do it well, you need to feel that your caregiver is on your side, that the relationship is nurturing for you as well as your child. Just as many parents leave a center because they feel the director is cool and insensitive as because they are dissatisfied with the way their child is cared for. Remember the emotional involvement we discussed in Chapter 2? You must feel that a caregiver belongs in your life, either as a friend or as a member of your extended family.

THE INTERVIEW

Now you're ready to begin the interview process. For your child, you will be looking at the person and the program (the kinds of things she plans to do with your child); for a day-care home or a center you will be looking at the setting as well.

Whatever kind of care you think you want, we recommend that you begin by spending a morning at a quality center in your area. Why? Because, when you choose a sitter or a nanny, you must rely on your impression of the *person* involved. Since you can't observe her, you are limited to what she *says* she does with kids. You have to educate yourself first—to learn what you need to ask. At a center you can watch caregivers and children together. In a group of eight to twelve toddlers or babblers or three- or four-year-olds, you'll get a sense of what the age group should be doing. You'll also be able to spot one or two who operate the way your child does. What kind of caregiver do they respond to and what do they like to do? Then when you talk to candidates for any kind of care, you'll have both general and specific questions to ask.

The best time to see a center is sometime after nine o'clock, when the children have had time to settle into their daily routine. (Not Monday: Mondays in child care, as in offices, are not prime time.) Mornings are best. From noon to two thirty you may run into rest periods, and after two thirty, you'll run into staff change-over and possibly the arrival of after-school kids (unless, of course, you're seeking that care).

If you are looking for infant care, ask a prospective sitter how she feels about talking to a baby. Most caregivers know enough to say they should cuddle infants. A lot of talking, however, is the surest indication that an infant is a real individual to her caregiver. Conversation, and lots of it, is also the foundation of language skills, critical in the first two to two-and-a-half years. (During a visit to a family day-care mother or center, you can watch to see if conversation is going on and assess the warmth or lack of it for yourself.)

For kids of all ages, but particularly for those around two, patience is an absolute requirement. Two-year-olds spend their time discovering, repeating, and testing in all areas, including that of independence. Their behavior is apt to be uneven—making great strides in some areas and none at all in others. They're not necessarily rewarding or easy to understand. Flexibility is another good quality in a caregiver for this age because no two days will be alike. Both qualities will make toilet training a more relaxed and less punitive step.

Remember that three- and four-year-olds are always in motion. They are beginning to follow directions, but they are still more apt to play than to sit still, so a caregiver must be play-oriented too, a person capable of childlike delight, who is good at drama and make-believe and folk songs and feels that she would wither in an office job. Mistakes are more apt to make her laugh than to upset her; she takes them in stride and goes on. Such people are usually pack rats, too—they hoard everything because egg cartons turned upside-down can become insects and paper plates can become Mother's Day plaques.

Since the children are grouped by age at a center, observe what is going on among them. Do the teachers encourage them to help one another and show them how to behave together? If one boy hits another on the back, does the teacher scold him, or does she say something like, "Are you trying to get Adam's attention? That's not the best way because it scares him. Try calling to him."

Parents worry about caregivers' physical drawbacks. They may be wary of older women, people with heavy foreign accents, too much weight, or disheveled appearances. If your child is at an age at which language development is crucial, an accent is a legitimate concern, since it may also imply poor command of the language. Does the overweight go hand in hand with a poor self-image?

Will that somehow carry over to the kids? Can an older woman really keep up with her charges? You have to watch. Do the children run to her? Are they eager to share what they are doing and do they listen to her? Is there lots of talk, whatever the accent?

There are certain background checks you must make of a nanny or sitter or day-care mother. In the initial phone call—whether you call in response to an ad or someone calls in response to yours —ask for references, complete with current addresses and phone numbers, and *pursue* them, explaining that you will call to set up an interview once you have talked to the references. That way you weed out unacceptable candidates and you know something about a candidate before you meet her. You'll also need some medical information, like the X ray mentioned earlier. Check her driving record if your state allows it. Does she live alone? have a family? You want some idea of how healthy her life would be, away from her job. If both parents are present, you'll give each other moral support. You may also find questions easier to ask if you write them down as a checklist.

This is the time to discuss specific duties and privileges. Do you expect her to shop for groceries? do the baby's laundry? the household laundry? get dinner? babysit in the evenings? How much time will she have off? Will she be able to use the car? How do you feel about her watching television? smoking? eating junk food? having friends over during the day? entertaining them in her room in the evening?

An essential: Build in flexibility whenever and wherever you can. Children grow and change; so do careers. Her job may need to change to fit. If this is your first adventure in babysitting and you are working parents, you don't yet know where the pressure points of your schedule will be. As one woman said, "You don't know what you don't know." It's best to begin with a trial period after which you can both reassess how her job should be structured. (Family laundry but not cooking the evening meal? Evening sitting once a week while the baby is still napping twice a day?)

Make sure you ask a day-care mother what arrangements she has made in case she becomes ill. Will finding an alternate be her job or yours? This is very important. If she accepts that responsibility, not only does it make your life much easier, but it is a clue that she takes her job seriously and knows what she is doing.

When you look at a center, you'll be looking at people with two different jobs. There will be teachers, akin to nannies or day-care mothers, who work directly with the children. *(Teacher* doesn't imply a degree in education, by the way—centers simply use the word because parents are familiar with it. Licensing agencies use the term *caregiver.* They are interchangeable.)

The center director (and her assistant, if she has one) is the other person for you to meet and form an opinion of. Her job is to relate to you, the parent, so we'll discuss what to look for in a separate section.

You look for many of the same qualities in a teacher in a center as you do in a sitter or a day-care mother, but there are some additional things to look for. Take note of the number of teachers. Are some children forced to stand in line for loving attention? (Teacher/child ratio throughout the industry averages one to ten; most states mandate a ratio of one to four or five for infants.) According to one study, a sign of a good center is that teachers and children share tasks such as setting up snacks or folding laundry together.

The most important indicator, we feel, is the relationship among the staff members. How long have the teachers been there? Do they work together with the relaxed give-and-take of mutual respect? When the director takes you on a tour, how does she talk to the teachers? How does she describe them? ("I'm blessed," said one director. You can't top that.) One mother made a suggestion we applaud. Always ask to use the staff bathroom. That's one of the few adult spaces at a center. If it's clean and well decorated, it's a sign of the staff's self-respect. Note the messages from management to staff. Are they clear and direct or punitive and demeaning?

The second area that concerns you is the *program,* the kinds of things a caregiver plans to do with your child. For infants, that is as simple as a daily report of eating, sleeping, and toileting schedules. (Since this little person is still pretty new to you, you need to know reactions to foods and why he came home sleepy on Tuesday but wide-eyed on Wednesday.) Quality centers do this routinely. If you decide on a nanny or on family day care, you might want to establish this kind of report yourself for the first few months.

What kinds of activities does the sitter/day-care mother/center plan for toddlers? For two-, three-, and four-year-olds? The days of children should not be rigidly organized, but the director should be able to describe activities that demonstrate that she knows the needs of each age. Activities should change with the seasons and occasions—awesome pumpkins for Halloween, sticky paper chains for Christmas, misspelled Father's Day cards. And they should make use of resources in your area, from the library to the firehouse to the hospital.

For older children, centers may have activities that include the whole family. There may be newsletters telling you of activities to ask about or to plan family adventures around. There may be open houses, even dinners for the whole center-based family—parents, center children, and siblings. Ask for a copy of the parent handbook if there is one.

When you choose group care outside your home, you become concerned with the *setting* as well as the person. One reflects the other. If a day-care mother has toys that are varied and challenging, that tells you that she is probably a stimulating caregiver. If she has piles of shells and yarn and empty egg cartons and the plastic blobs used in shipping, you can induce that she is a project-minded pack rat. If her house looks drab and uninviting, that tells you that she may not be the person with whom you want your child to spend his days.

In general, though, you are inspecting a day-care home for safety—safety caps in electrical outlets, sound furniture, fire extinguisher and an escape route in case of fire, gates at the head and foot of stairs. Is the paint in good condition? Is it lead-based? What is the bathroom like? Where do the children eat and where are they changed? Is the number of the nearest poison-control center posted near the phone?

Whatever the kind or size of the center, you will look for the same safety standards. But there will be others as well. First of all, the license should be displayed. A license isn't a guarantee of quality, but a center must meet the standards discussed in Chapter 1 to earn one, so the absence of a license is a red flag. The week's menus should also be posted. There's also a sign that means you should turn and leave immediately: one that states that parents must call ahead before they visit. You *must* be free to drop in any time. (And remember to do it!)

Other pointers: Are the center's rooms light and airy? The more open the architecture, the better the built-in protection from child abuse because teachers and director will oversee one another. Since a center serves more children than a day-care home, you'll be more concerned about the bathrooms—are they clean and are there enough of them? Are the toilets child-sized and the sinks installed at a child's height? What about decorations? Is there plenty of children's artwork pinned up? Is it recent and is it posted at the kids' eye level? Are there photographs of families? Outdoors, is the equipment sturdy enough to challenge the older kids, and is there a separate, much quieter area for infants and toddlers to be outside without being stampeded by the big kids? Can the director explain how the play area for two-year-olds differs from that for three-year-olds, four-year-olds, and, again, school-agers?

If you are looking for infant care, the infant area should be separate from the rest of the center, with a glassed-in wall or door so that the director can monitor it easily. Your child should have her own crib. The changing area should be far away from any eating area. Look for soap and rubber gloves in the changing area; if a teacher is changing a baby, pause to see how thoroughly she washes her hands afterward.

All these things are essential because cleanliness is essential. But if that's all an infant area offers, it can mean a warehouse of thirty cribs in rows, sterile and boring. Look too for coziness—mirrors at floor level, bright colors, lots of toys that dangle and jangle, lots of soft interesting noises and music.

DON'T FORGET YOUR OWN NEEDS

Just as you look at how caregivers meet your child's needs, look at how they might meet your own. Again, it's valuable to talk to a center director because she is trained to respond to what you need. That doesn't commit you to a center as a final choice, but it will improve the choice you do make.

You may never have the time to become friends with your caregiver, but you should have the feeling that friendship is possible. Why? Because she gives you the feeling that she's a listener. That she cares about the same things about children that you care about. You feel that you might be able to relax and trust her enough to discuss problems and share concerns, however awkward. (If you are to share your child's growth, there will be many awkward discussions.) Since she knows her business better than you do, she should point out strengths she has to offer that you haven't even thought of.

Two attitudes will indicate this during an interview. The first is a caregiver's attitude toward both parents working. Look for clear approval. When there's disapproval, it's generally directed toward the mother—even though the caregiver is almost certainly a working mother herself. She may resent having to work or there may even be a philosophical or religious conviction. Whatever the reason, you don't want your child to spend his days with somebody whose unspoken attitude is "You poor thing, your mother neglects you. She works." And you won't ask for or listen to advice from someone sending out waves of disapproval.

You also have a right not to be judged. One mother of a hyperactive child failed to tell any of the centers she interviewed that he was taking ritalin because she feared they wouldn't accept him. Every child and every family has quirks. You need to feel comfortable sharing full information, knowing that it won't be held against you but will help a caregiver to work with you. That's the attitude you're looking for. If a caregiver is too judgmental, consider it a warning bell.

You should discuss child-rearing issues with any potential caregiver. The most important one is probably how she feels about discipline and how she manages a child's behavior. A caregiver may discipline at times you would not, in ways that would never occur to you. Some otherwise loving caregivers believe in curing a child who bites by biting him back, tying a restless child in bed at naptime, threatening to call the police or "whupping" misbehaving children with electrical cords. It happens, and it's better to find out about their philosophy during the interview than from your frightened child. Sometimes parents ask for discipline that a caregiver can't (or shouldn't) follow. Parents frequently give caregivers permission to spank their children. In most states, centers are forbidden by law to use corporal punishment. You put any caregiver in a precarious legal position by requesting it.

The caregiver you choose may well be the one to guide your child's first steps and catch the first loose tooth. We'll deal with your feelings about that elsewhere. What you need to know when you interview is if a caregiver is sensitive to your sense of loss. Ask the sitter, day-care mother, or center director how she feels about calling you at work when a milestone of growth occurs. (Some centers do this as a matter of policy, by the way.) If her eyes light up, you know that she understands and values your concerns. If she agrees so politely that it's clear she doesn't know what you're talking about, you know that she doesn't.

If a center teacher's appearance or accent disturbs you, that is also something to discuss with the director. It's very difficult to do. But the director should be alert to your concerns. Perhaps she'll explain to you that Miss Susan, though overweight, is outgoing and confident and has boundless energy. Perhaps she'll point out to you that the children have other teachers besides Miss Inez, so that she is not their only source of language, and she'll ask you to watch how the children run to her and trust her.

Other issues that are special to some parents: how a caregiver feels about single parents, whether girls and boys are treated differently, how much parent participation is allowed (or required), and whether there will be any religious guidance. Write down your concerns ahead of time and just go down the list.

MAKING THE DECISION

It's best if both parents can be present at an interview, or at least pay a visit prior to enrollment. Each will have a different set of criteria; each will notice things that escape the other. In any case, push yourself to check out two or three sources in each category available to you.

The most common trap of any kind of child care search is settling—making your decision before you have seen enough caregivers and settings to make a good choice. (One of the biggest pluses of working through an agency may be that they help you avoid that.) It's partly the reluctance to seem rude, partly the fear that while you keep on looking, the sitter may take another job or the center or family day-care mother fill their spaces. Unfortunately, that might happen. Quality child care of any kind is in great demand today. Corporate and state studies regularly report three to four parents looking for every spot available; for infant care the figure is even higher. If an applicant doesn't actually leer in a sinister manner, the temptation is great to say, she'll do, at least till I find something better.

Don't do it. For one thing, it's never wise to make a choice on the spot. Impressions you weren't aware of at the time may filter through later, often in the middle of the night, and if they don't for you, they may for your partner.

Then, too, we find that people have trouble leaving child care, even bad care. It's hard to admit that you've made a poor choice for your child. You make excuses, you ignore bad signs—and who can blame you, when you dread a second search and have no reason to expect it to be more successful than the first? If you're in emergency mode and can't afford to wait the two to three weeks that a successful search usually requires, turn to one of the sources we describe in Chapter 8, "Once-in-a-While Care," to tide you over.

When you have winnowed your choices down to a few, it's time to bring your child into the process. Don't ask him to meet somebody as a possible caregiver—it's too much for a child to handle—but ask the person to come as a sitter for a Saturday afternoon or evening so that you can see her in a care-giving, as opposed to an interview, situation. Make no commitments beforehand. Revisit the day-care homes or centers at the top of your list, this time with your child. Some parents even arrange to spend a morning. It's a question of what gives you the greatest peace of mind.

In the end, it's up to you.

Good luck. The adventure is about to begin.

PART TWO

DAY IN AND DAY OUT

The time has come to settle into child care. Buckling your toddler into his car seat for the drive to his child care center or welcoming the sitter to your house are about to become habits, Monday through Friday, week after week, more cheerful some days than others, but nevertheless habits. On good days you may even do something you never thought you would do again—relax. And so you should. It's your reward for having chosen well.

Once you've heaved that sigh of relief, though, you'll realize very quickly that child care is more than a single decision, however wisely made. You're now in a new, uncharted land—living with child care.

Living with the routine of child care, keeping it ticking in a way satisfying to all concerned, is something parents know little about. All too many assume that, while they'll be told if

. . . .

something goes drastically wrong, if all is well, their role consists of writing a weekly check to the child care provider. Some parents feel guilty about that, others resentful, still others relieved.

Few understand just how wrong the assumption is. The fact is, child care leaves its mark, on your child and on your family. Your child will learn things he might not learn at home; he will handle many milestones of childhood differently.

In Part Two we'll be discussing what it's like to live with child care day in and day out—how to put your best foot forward as you begin the routines of child care, what happens to a child's patterns of eating and sleeping and play when he spends his days in child care, the most common disagreements that develop in each kind of care, and how to find the care you need only now and then—to cover for illness or while traveling.

There will be changes in your life too. There's no need to mourn the changes—we think many of them are enriching—but we do think you need to recognize what's happening. If you want child care to work well for you, then learn how to work well with it. You may not know how to do that now, but at the end of Part Two, you will.

PUTTING YOUR BEST FOOT FORWARD

. . . .

Congratulations on your decision, whatever it was. Make a point of celebrating in some way—all of you, including your child—both because it sets the right tone of anticipation and because you won't get another chance to enjoy your feeling of relief. The next step looms immediately: actually embarking on child care.

There are several steps involved. First, there is the preparation beforehand—thinking through what you want done and when and how. At centers (and often in family day care) there is a registration procedure at which policies and mutual responsibilities will be spelled out. Then there is the big day itself. You will want to beware of some of the easy-to-avoid mistakes many parents make in the beginning, simply because they aren't familiar with the etiquette of child care. And finally, we have suggestions on how to begin a positive relationship with your caregiver, both for you and for your child.

PAPERWORK, POLICIES, AND PROCEDURES

Your first official step into child care will be taking care of paperwork. If you are working with an agency or a center or in some instances a day-care mother, there will be forms to fill out. If some of the paperwork seems needlessly bureaucratic, try to remember that your child care provider is every bit as aware as you are of the precious burden you are entrusting to her. The provider is your proxy in your absence, and she knows by now the contingencies that need to be covered ahead of time.

The forms generally cover two different areas. The first is information—the name you prefer your child to be called; any special needs (food allergies, for example); your office phone numbers; someone who can be called in case of emergency. It's a good idea to review the parent handbook with the director at this time. Know what your commitments are.

The second area is the enrollment agreement, which you will be asked to sign. Read it carefully. It will state the hours the center is open; the policy regarding such things as illness, bringing in food or toys, and discipline; your permission to have your child given medical treatment in case of emergency; and, last but not least, terms of payment—how much, when, and to whom. Payment is nearly always weekly, paid in advance. If your child goes in for a single day and spends the rest of the week home ill or away on holiday, you'll still be asked to pay tuition for the full week. You are usually asked to pay with cash or personal check (unless a check bounces, in which case cash will be required); credit cards probably won't be allowed. There will be extra fees if you are late picking up your child.

As you can see, it's a good idea to have terms of employment spelled out instead of assumed, regardless of your choice of care. A sitter might be intimidated by something that seemed too official, however. Our advice is that, once you have hired a sitter, you send her a letter saying how pleased you are that she is coming—and incidentally repeating the tasks and terms that you have discussed. Then, if there has been a misunderstanding, you can work it out ahead of time.

Permission slips are another important piece of paperwork. Many states require that centers have permission slips before taking a child on a field trip (zoo, museum, pumpkin farm), and sometimes day-care mothers as well. If you are placing your child in a center, the application may include a permission slip for any field trips, followed by specific releases for each trip.

A center will ask you to provide a medical record (and if you're not asked, think twice about your choice because this is a state requirement for a license). A good medical record includes your child's immunization shots, as well as any medical quirks—sensitivity to penicillin, allergies, any medications taken regularly, a tendency to get ear infections. Prepare similar records for a sitter or day-care mother. If your child ever requires emergency care, these records will be needed.

In the case of an infant, your caregiver will want to know how much he eats, when he naps and for how long, if he fusses for a given period each day, and whether he has a regular pattern of bowel movements. In the case of a toddler, you might want to pass on pet food hates. (Then if your caregiver succeeds in getting him to try them, she'll let you know!)

Tell your pediatrician who your caregiver is, including phone number, and tell your caregiver who your pediatrician is, including phone number. If you rely on an outpatient clinic instead of a pediatrician, as many parents do, say so.

Whether your caregiver is a sitter, day-care mother, or center director, she must know that she can call either parent at work and that the parent will accept the call. Your office phone number is on the form, but that's only half of it. It's your job to give your child care provider's name to your secretary, receptionist, or whoever tends your office phone. You will also need to make it clear that she *must* be put through when she calls.

Who can visit the center or day-care home and observe your child? Who can pick him up? The other parent, if you are divorced? (Both parents have legal access to their child unless the caregiver has a notarized court order stating otherwise.) Grandparents? Other relatives? A neighbor? Provide a list of names and keep it up to date—the center or day-care mother shouldn't release your child to anybody else. (By the way, the people on the list may have to show identification when they visit or pick up your child.) Parents in big cities find this protection reassuring; parents in the rest of the country are generally uncomfortable. But it is a legal and safety precaution everybody needs.

Your list of names must include at least one emergency backup —somebody who can be called in case your child suddenly spikes a fever and must be picked up. Do remember to inform whomever you've chosen as emergency backup (including her need to show identification), particularly if you are working out of town.

HELPING YOUR CHILD HANDLE THE FIRST FEW DAYS

Next comes the big day itself.

Your attitude toward this new experience will set the tone for your child. An infant is too young to understand what you say, but he can easily pick up the difference between "I'm abandoning you" and "Something exciting is happening to you today." Toddlers on up, of course, can understand the words as well. Your guilt or unhappiness will make his adjustment much more difficult, so if you feel either, try to keep your emotions to yourself. Don't gush —children probably pick up on false notes faster than adults do. Think of how you would describe a new job opportunity—a combination of nervousness and anticipation. That's a mix your child will be able to understand readily because he no doubt feels that way himself.

For this first day (and probably for the first week), your child's adjustment to child care may be more important than your job, so plan ahead for this period. Take vacation days in half days, trade shifts with co-workers, or alternate days with your husband or wife.

With your child, plan the kind of clothes he should wear. Layers are best—then he can easily take off or add to be as cool or warm as he needs to be throughout the day. Pack a diaper bag or backpack (or set out supplies if you have in-home care), explaining what each thing is for. The pack should contain a complete change of clothes—more than one for an infant or a child in the midst of toilet training—in case he gets wet playing; plenty of outdoor gear; and a favorite toy or blanket, at least for the first few days. (Even if Teddy has to stay in the backpack, your child will know he's close by.) For most day-care mothers and some centers, you'll need to pack a lunch. And everything—show him with pride— marked with *his name!*

On that first day, plan to arrive later than nine o'clock, after the bustle of regular arrivals is over, and plan to stay at least an hour. Involve yourself unobtrusively. Pour juice, set out blocks, help kids off with boots. When your child seems settled in, tell him matter-of-factly that you are leaving, and then go quickly. Don't try to sneak out, in other words, but don't make so much fuss that he feels honor-bound to get upset too.

In the afternoon, reverse the process. Pick him up about four, before the mass exodus, allowing time to stay and watch for a while if he is involved in some play. In fact, encourage him to continue playing for a few minutes—it tells him that you feel at home. In any case, you'll want to chat with the day-care mother or center teacher about what happened that day. ("You won't believe this, but today Esmeralda asked us if she could help serve snack!" or "Wait till you see the fingerpainting Jeffrey did today!")

Talk about his day that night—not probing questions that put him on the spot (did you like it?) but casual ones (who did you play with today? what did you have for lunch? did you feel sleepy after lunch?). The conversation will be easier if you share your day too. When one mother asked, "What do you think I was doing today?" her daughter said complacently, "Missing me." Right from the start, you want your attitude to say, not that you have been isolated from each other all day but that now he has "his" place just as work is "yours."

In our experience, almost all children let you leave more willingly when it is crystal clear to them that you are willing to stay. It's one of the Catch-22's of parenting. Still, you will probably want to keep up this beginning routine for a few days, gradually shortening the time until by the end of the week you are arriving and leaving at the same time as the other parents. In the second week, switch to a normal schedule.

Most children take two to three weeks to settle in, but the range is great. Gregarious children may take off without a backward look, leaving their parents feeling a bit downcast. Some children seem smooth as silk for a week or so—or even six months or so—*then* fuss, as though testing whether you are really serious about this new routine. A few can take as long as three months to settle in. That doesn't mean they wail from eight in the morning till six at night for three months, but children who find it very hard to adapt to new things may have lingering tearful episodes scattered through the days when they abruptly remember where they are—or, rather, where they are not.

If this happens to your child, keep checking with the sitter or the center director. A child having trouble with this separation (particularly at about a year) needs to be held a lot—perhaps constantly for a few days. One director put an unhappy boy in a little red wagon and pulled him with her everywhere for a week till he settled in. You have a right to this kind of consideration.

For older children who are slow settling in, ask for examples of play each day, ask for the names of the children he spends the most time with and try to meet the parents—perhaps you could arrange a play time on the weekend at your house. But if you feel confident that the child care setting is a good one and you know your child has trouble adapting to anything new, remember that stopping halfway through his adjustment won't necessarily solve anything. If you switch to a sitter at home, that now becomes the strange situation. If you move to a new child care setting, that too is a strange situation. He'll just have to begin the lengthy process of adapting all over again.

DOING YOUR PART RIGHT FROM THE START

The way you handle these first few days and weeks will make up your caregiver's first impressions of you. Since you are embarking on what you hope will be a long-term relationship, it makes sense to put your best foot forward—not to make any mistakes you could easily avoid.

Some common ones fall into a category that might be called etiquette. For example, be prompt. If you're taking your child to a day-care home or child care center, arrive when you said you would. Promptness at the end of the day is perhaps even more important. Whether you are picking up your child or arriving home to relieve a babysitter, being fifteen minutes late repeatedly signals lack of respect. (Once you're there, though, lingering to chat is acceptable, even welcome.) If your caregiver is a by-the-hour sitter or a relative or a day-care mother, she may find it difficult to charge you for fifteen minutes, but she'll resent it just the same. At some day-care homes and most centers you'll be charged steeply for minor daily lateness. That's how offensive caregivers find this habit.

Be prompt, too, about paying. At the interview you discussed how and when to pay as well as how much. Now follow through on your agreement to the letter. No excuses.

If you have in-home care, the biggest pitfall is the temptation to extend her job. When you hired your housekeeper or nanny or sitter, you discussed what household tasks would be included and what the hours would be. Whatever you agreed upon, that's it. Like petty lateness, petty additions to her job quickly build into big trouble. One agency that works with girls from the Midwest agreed that it's the principal reason relationships founder.

A similar abuse in center-based care is asking teachers to babysit on evenings and weekends. Of course, it would be jam for you. If you had to work late, the teacher could take your child home with her, and you could pick him up at your convenience. And if you had to travel or you and your spouse wanted to get away for a private weekend . . . but centers don't want some children to think of themselves as special or other children to be envious when they see the favored few arrive or leave with a teacher. A director may not be able to forbid babysitting (though they can forbid teachers to leave with children), but the director won't be pleased. And the disadvantage to you is that your child's babysitter has already worked an eight-hour day.

The question also arises at a center: Who do you talk to about what? You are always dealing with at least three people—your child's eight-to-three o'clock teacher, the part-time teacher who relieves her in the afternoon, and the director (and/or her assistant). Each handles a different aspect of the child care relationship.

Many parents get off on the wrong foot here. They ask a teacher for a permission she is not supposed to give—and she may grant it anyway; this leads to confusion. Parents often ask a teacher to clarify a policy—and if it's beyond the scope of her job, she may not do so accurately. They make a complaint to a teacher assuming she will talk to the director—and either the teacher assumes the parent has done so (stalemate) or she reacts with hurt or defensiveness.

As we said earlier, teachers are responsible for the relationship with your child. Your child will always have more than one teacher over the course of his ten- or eleven-hour day. If you're happy and stay there for years, he'll move from one teacher to another during that time.

The director (and her assistant) are responsible for the relationship with *you*. She provides the continuity; she will be the one who knows you—and whom you know—over time. She is the one with whom you talk and discuss concerns and problems. This is not going behind the teacher's back. The director sets up the schedule for herself and her assistant with this purpose in mind: One or the other will always be present at drop-off and pick-up times, ready for the quick casual conversations that are the best way to keep minor problems from becoming major ones. Three times a year you'll meet formally with both director and teacher(s) to review your child's developmental progress.

Another area in which you must do your part right from the start is in the way you handle your child's inevitable illnesses. (This one may come up almost immediately because your child is being exposed to a whole family of new germs. But most children don't get sick.)

There are regulations and policies regarding illness. If you signed an agreement, it almost certainly included a provision against bringing your child in when he's ill. The common policy is usually along these lines: A child with only sniffles is accepted without comment. If a child has a fever of a hundred degrees or more, the center director or day-care mother will probably call the parent. If he has been home sick, and it is his first day back and he spikes a fever in the afternoon, she'll tell the parent at pick-up time. If there's a high fever, she'll call and say, "When can you or your designated back-up person be here?" If there is a convulsion or an injury, such as a bad fall from a piece of playground equipment, she will probably call a paramedic with an emergency vehicle. In other words, nobody in the child care business wants to take the responsibility for diagnosing or caring for a sick child.

States don't want them to, either. In many states, a caregiver cannot even give a child acetaminophen unless it is prescribed. Many centers will give a child only one dose daily, again prescribed by a physician. If it's a four-times-a-day antibiotic or medicated cough syrup, they'll administer the noon dose, leaving early morning, six o'clock, and bedtime for the parent. Ask your pharmacist to make up a separate bottle for your caregiver, complete with instructions and the doctor's name. And get a fresh bottle each time. A center won't keep medication beyond the period of illness, and neither should you.

Even when there is nothing spelled out on paper, it's still a bad practice to take a sick child outdoors, drive him to a sitter's house, and expect him to spend the day trying to keep up with healthy, active kids. Ask any pediatrician or caregiver. A child with sniffles probably does no harm to himself or anyone else. If a child is feverish and really not feeling well, however, he should stay home. In almost all cases, he'll bounce back within twenty-four to forty-eight hours, either because he's over whatever he had or because an antibiotic has begun to take effect and the pediatrician has given you the go-ahead to send him back.

If a child does come in while he's feverish, three things will probably happen: He will pass his germs on to every other child in the day-care home or child care center; in his vulnerable state, he will be much more susceptible to whatever germs others are carrying; and as he tries to keep up with the activities of everybody else, he will invariably get sicker and have to stay home longer than if he had been kept home a day or two at the outset.

In order to avoid the illness trap, it's important to line up an emergency backup from the very beginning, even if you don't need the help for months. (See "Once-in-a-While Care," page 109.)

BUILDING A GOOD RELATIONSHIP WITH YOUR CAREGIVER

A third area, just as important as the first two, is to begin the relationship with your caregiver in a way that you can build on.

It may comfort you to know that most parents have trouble striking the right note. In general, parents begin by expecting caregivers to be more consistent than is humanly possible. You want a caregiver who will never scream about spilled food or cry after a day with a whiny child or commit any of the other parenting sins that you have been known to commit yourself upon occasion. On the other hand, you want a caregiver to do all the good things that you do—make a fuss about a pretty dress, hug and kiss lavishly, ooh and aah when spoon succeeds in finding mouth.

Given the eleven or so hours a day you need child care, you're not going to get that kind of perfection day in and day out. If you have a single caregiver—nanny or day-care mother—she'll be tired by evening, just as you would be. If you choose a center, your eleven hours will automatically include more than one caregiver. There will be bad days along with good, raised voices, and turnover of employees. If you see any of these, of course, ask questions —Bad day? Is somebody sick?—but don't accuse. In other words, make it clear that you've seen the behavior but that you're aware there may be a good explanation. And if there *is* an explanation (she had two wisdom teeth pulled yesterday; we just learned that Eric is moving to Kansas and the children are sad today) try to show the same understanding you would like someone to extend to you.

Parents also have trouble simply talking to caregivers—expressing satisfaction without sounding patronizing or talking about something that isn't going well without sounding overly critical or even just talking about what happened that day. Some parents breeze in and breeze out again, never saying much, with an attitude that's equally easy to interpret either as "Everything is going well" or "I don't give a damn how it's going." Other parents talk to the caregiver but not directly about their child. If a newspaper article appears on child care, this parent compares its results with her own care. If a new study on child development appears, she will make a photocopy for the provider to read. If a parents' advisory committee is formed, she is on it, and probably suggested it.

The best first impression as far as a caregiver is concerned springs from the relationship she sees between you and your child. If it's warm and caring, if she sees you taking the time to show interest in your child's day, if your talk with her is rooted in the events of his day, she will assume that you can all work together. Child care providers go out of their way for this kind of parent, as teachers will too in the years to come, and no wonder!

Another way to begin the relationship on a sound footing is to make it clear that you know your child will become fond of his caregiver, and that you accept and want that to happen. If you've done a good job in choosing your caregiver, your child is going to love her. If you've done a good job in helping your child anticipate child care, he's going to trust her. No, not as he loves you, his parents, but as another member of the family. And you must nurture that shared love and trust from the very beginning.

Here is the kind of thing we are talking about. When there is a birthday in your child's group, ask your caregiver when *her* birthday is; make a note of it, and when the day comes, give her a card or wish her happy birthday. When she tells you about something interesting or funny that your child has done, comment on her insight. If your child's hair is freshly combed at the end of the day, that matters to you; if you thank her for it, that matters to her. When your child runs to her and hugs her after she's been away on vacation or ill, tell her how happy it makes you to see the love between them.

We will talk about this relationship in detail throughout the book. For now, think of it this way: You know the importance of good child care to your family's life. Once you've found it, don't fight it. You want to be able to say to your caregiver, "My child loves you. And I love you because you love my child."

This does not mean overlooking anything that troubles you, of course. A good caregiver wants you to talk about things that don't seem to be working as well as those that do. If your child's sleep patterns have changed since the onset of child care, if he has always eaten a good dinner and now suddenly he doesn't, if he seems noticeably noisier, talk about it. Don't wait for incidents to fester —if you do, your resentment will be all out of proportion to the importance of what you are talking about. That's another reason we recommend planning to spend fifteen minutes with your caregiver at pick-up time. Most nights you may simply watch your child play or chat with other mothers (both valuable activities, by the way). Most nights there will be only good things to talk about. But when you need to talk to your caregiver or she needs to talk to you, those talks too will be merely another non-threatening part of the routine. (Your child should not be present at these conversations.)

HELPING YOUR CHILD CARE FOR HIS CAREGIVER

Help your child get off on the right foot too. Does your caregiver have favorite books and games? Have them on hand when she arrives. Does a center teacher use a hand signal to ask children to be still at Circle Time or a password to tell them to line up to go outdoors? Teach it to him beforehand. When your caregiver mentions something positive at the end of the day, repeat it with great gusto, in your child's presence, to your spouse. Maybe Esmeralda could serve you juice tonight too.

Make it clear too that you assume he will misbehave sometimes. That doesn't mean asking, "Did you do anything bad today?" but occasionally, "What does Miss Mary do when she gets angry?" The "when" is very important; it tells your child that you know and accept the fact that he will misbehave from time to time. And be alert to *his* comments. "Miss Mary doesn't like me" doesn't mean Miss Mary doesn't like him, it means he has misbehaved; that's the perfect moment for "What does Miss Mary do *when* she's angry?"

Understanding your responsibilities and helping your child settle in will help all of you make a good start. But it is only the start. Living with child care will mean other changes, which we'll talk about in the next chapter.

THE RIPPLE EFFECT
OF THE CHILD CARE DAY

. . . .

When she gets hungry, when she gets tired, when she goes outdoors—habits like these mark the hours of your child's day. Once you are over the initial excitement of embarking on child care and the family has begun to settle into a routine, some, possibly most, of these routines will change—and you'll find to your surprise that the changes ripple through the family as well.

The age of your child is a factor, of course. If you have an infant and are starting right out with child care, she will have child care-compatible habits from the very beginning, and you'll never spare a thought for what you might have done differently if you'd been at home. And if you've chosen child care wisely, her habits will be handled in the early months much as you would have done yourself. She'll be fed and changed as she needs to be. She'll be talked to; she'll be taken outside. If she's in group care, her naptime will be influenced by the center's or day-care mother's schedule and may fall at a time you might not have chosen, but since you won't be there, that won't trouble you. You and your caregiver will exchange information about the patterns of eating and sleeping she is developing, and you will exchange stories of the wondrous things she has done. And since infants are enchanting, and you are both in love with her, you won't find much to disagree about.

When your child is between one and two years old, the scene shifts. By this age, almost all parents want their children involved in some form of group care, whether it's just part of their child care plan—a play group a few afternoons each week, a toddler exercise group, half-day nursery school—or whether they place their children in all-day center care. And that's when the impact of child care will be felt.

Once your child is in group care, there *will be* changes. Her daily routine will be set by somebody else, and some of that routine—probably to your surprise—will be guided by state regulations.

Please note that we have said that your child's habits will change without adding adjectives like *good* or *bad*. It's important for your family's sanity to remember right from the start that the changes are neither good nor bad: they're inevitable. If you try to ignore them, they'll take place just the same, and you will also complicate your child's life by forcing her to divide her life into a Monday-to-Friday world and a weekend world. For small children, that can be quite a stress.

If, on the other hand, you absorb and adapt to these changes as most parents do, your family's life will change too. We're going to walk through the biggest changes with you, showing why they happen, what the effects on the family's life will be, plus suggestions for turning them to your advantage. As you and your child and your child care provider begin to work together, child care will move from the add-on to your family to an integral part of all your lives, as much a plus for your child as your job is for you.

WHEN, WHAT, AND HOW MUCH YOUR CHILD EATS

We'll talk about your child's eating patterns first because this is nearly always the change parents notice first. If you have in-home care, you probably assume that the menu is under your control, but this is not always the case. Your caregiver may have more casual ideas of nutrition than you do, and the corn chips you bought for a snack may be lunch, followed by ice cream for dessert. You may want your child to eat everything on her plate, and your caregiver may shunt two-thirds of it into the garbage disposal without telling you. Or you may be the one with a relaxed attitude toward what your child eats, while the sitter feels that if your child doesn't eat everything, she hasn't done her job.

Try to avoid making eating a pressure point if you can. You can avoid junk food by simply not having it in the house. If you have a fussy eater, try asking the sitter what she feeds her own children and add it to the lunch list—she may push her own choices harder, and if your child reaches kindergarten wise in the ways of quiche or cajun food, so much the better. If you aren't fussy, be sure you make that very clear. Child and sitter can get locked into a struggle about food just as child and parent can, and one habit is just as bad as the other.

If your child is in a family day-care home, whether it's licensed or not, you probably send in a brown bag lunch. Again, you have control over the menu. Your choices are narrower than when you have access to your own kitchen; you're restricted by what still looks and tastes appealing after several hours. You'll never know how much is eaten or whether your careful slices of raw vegetables were traded for somebody else's Oreos. There's also the added task of making the lunch, either in the evenings when you're tired or in the mornings when you're rushed.

If your child is in a center, in some states you can still send in a brown bag lunch, but in most cases the menus come under state control, in both large ways and small. For example, the number of meals—midmorning snack, hot lunch, afternoon snack—is mandated by many states. Menus must be approved by most states so that a certain level of nutrition is guaranteed. These requirements may be quite detailed. In Ohio, for example, juice must be single-strength juice rather than a punch with a fruit juice base, and you can't mix flavors—no apple plus grape.

Increasingly, centers are moving beyond state mandates to serve breakfast as well because so many parents ask them to. This is partly because people are becoming more realistic about their own schedules. If you have a long drive to work, as most people in Houston do, for example, you're not up to fixing a big breakfast at six in the morning. Parents are also becoming more realistic about their children, who are not ready to tumble out of bed and eat that big breakfast immediately even if parents had time to cook it. A glass of juice will tide her over while you dress her and yourself; by the time you drop her off at the center, she is wide awake and hungry. Centers that don't serve breakfast have begun to beef up their morning snack from juice and a cracker, say, to a piece of French toast or a biscuit with honey.

That doesn't sound like your child? Ah. Now we come to the second part of the equation, which is how your child's eating habits will change when she eats some place other than your house.

Your pediatrician could weigh your daughter and reassure you daily about her weight, but in some corner of your mind you would still know that to be healthy, she needs to eat a sandwich for lunch each day. By sandwich, you mean two slices of bread plus filling. If a quarter sandwich is all she ever nibbles away, you are left with a daily worry. Is she growing properly? Should you try another brand of tuna fish? Will she be more susceptible to colds? (Are you a good mother?) Should you reward/bribe her with a cookie?

If you have a finicky eater, this daily struggle over food is not minor. It can easily set a parent/child pattern that will haunt you long after calories no longer count. We have heard parents contemplate Florida vacations not because of Walt Disney World but because they think their kids might eat more where it's hot and sunny. By the time a family has reached that point, what began as a concern for health has turned into a power struggle—one, moreover, that the child can always win.

That doesn't mean that a finicky eater is a manipulative child—she may be unable to help herself. Allergies frequently play a role. Pediatricians are reluctant to do extensive testing for food allergies in children since it is an expensive, unpleasant process and children outgrow most food allergies anyway. Still, if allergies mean that much of what a child eats makes her uncomfortable, it stands to reason that she will be cautious about what she tries and won't look forward to mealtime. Allergies or not, if a child fusses about food, almost without realizing it, the family menus dwindle to what she will eat without protest.

Day-care homes and centers have quite a different attitude. They, like your pediatrician, will be relaxed about the kinds and amounts of food your child actually eats. The amount your daughter eats in child care may not change, but the emotional overtones are gone. Food ceases to be either a stress or a power struggle.

Then too, the dietician who plans a center's menus and the state regulator who approves them have much more experience than you do with what kids really will eat. That means lots of noodle-y casseroles, finger foods, and sliced fresh fruit and vegetables. It's child-oriented food, and if you have a finicky eater, it's probably a wider range of choices than you have been offering at home.

The mealtime atmosphere too is entirely different in a day-care home or a center. Instead of a sedate one-on-one meal with you or a sitter, it's a jumbled social event just this side of *Animal House*. Instead of the lengthy and often tense period when you teach your child to accept solid food, to go from mush to bite sizes, to handle a spoon, she watches children a few months older and copies them when she's ready. Not only is it painless, but she will experience a terrific feeling of mastery: her triumph rather than her acceptance of your idea. She eats a broader range of foods because it's easier to go along with what everybody else is eating than to say an automatic "I don't like it." Children at centers regularly snack on—are you ready for this?—broccoli and celery. (We overheard a teacher inviting a group of not-quite-two-year-olds: "Would you like to taste a *real* grape?")

By the time you pick her up in the evening, then, your daughter has had the opportunity to eat a midmorning snack, a hot lunch, a midafternoon snack, and possibly breakfast as well, each one in a heady social atmosphere.

Of course, it's reassuring to realize how well she's being taken care of—if she's picky, it's a great relief as well. But the effects on your family life are more far-reaching than that. What happens, for example, if you serve dinner at your old, pre–child care dinner hour of five thirty or six? Your child won't be able to eat. She's not expressing hostility toward you for putting her in child care, and she's not turning up her nose at your choice of food. She's just not hungry. If she's picky, there may be days she eats less and days she eats more, but she may go for weeks without wanting or needing much more for dinner than a bowl of cereal, and she may not even want that until close to bedtime.

The change in her eating habits is inevitable, for all the reasons we've listed above. To try to fight it is to turn your evening hours together into a long and meaningless power struggle.

If, instead, you try to work with her new eating pattern, what happens? Your family's evenings will change, with the degree of change varying from one family to the next. Here's how it works.

Since centers are required to post weekly menus, you can always find out in advance what your child will be served. If your child is a healthy eater and you know she will be getting most of what she needs during the day, can you and your husband do the same—get good hot meals at lunch at your workplaces? If so, why not rethink your evening meal? It's true that dinnertime was an important event in "Leave It to Beaver" and "Ozzie and Harriet," but times change. Think what a great relief it would be to the family cook, and even the budget, if instead of a full meal you had a cheese and veggy snack for the early evening. If that's not enough for you, after your child is in bed, enjoy the luxury of an adult, uninterrupted, unhurried meal.

If you have a finicky eater, the change won't be as great. Then you check the menus for the days when special favorites are served, plan light suppers for those days, and give yourself a break. This period is a brief one. By the time your child is four or five, she'll be ready for dinner at the end of the day. But for these few years, plan evening meals that fit your child's and your needs rather than somebody else's ideal.

Something else happens when dinner loses its role as a central family time: You get to replace it however you choose. When necessary, you can do errands without feeling guilty for depriving your child. You can water the grass, stop by to visit grandma for an hour or two, or sweep the front walk. At six in the evening, you would have the zoo to yourself. The sky (well, bedtime) is the limit.

WHEN YOUR CHILD'S SLEEP HABITS CHANGE

Eating patterns will probably be the greatest change in your child's habits, but her patterns of sleeping will also be affected by child care, for similar reasons. You may have been keeping your toddler awake and occupied through her former naptime so that she'd go to bed earlier. Now she's in child care and you find that bedtime is dragging out and becoming a whiny, fussy, thoroughly unpleasant time. Why? Because she's napping again.

There is very little you can do about it. State regulations stipulate that children must have a regular rest period during the day, from one to two and a half hours, depending on the state. The stipulation reads *rest,* not *sleep*—children must be on their mats or cots, but they can have a book, or a teacher may read to them. But a busy child may need her nap each day, so even if you ask the teacher to keep her awake to preserve her bedtime, it may not be possible. Even if she does not sleep, she is rested when you pick her up in the evening.

Again, bear in mind that this period is short. By four or five, when children no longer nap and spend their rest period reading, your child will be ready for an earlier bedtime. For now, though, you cannot successfully enforce the bedtime hour you have been used to. You can follow the lead of child care centers and allow your child to take a book to bed, or you may consciously choose to have some kind of vigorous play early in the evening to tire her. Or, with the extra time freed from cooking and setting the table for a formal dinner, knowing she is neither tired nor hungry, you may decide to turn routine shopping into a slower-paced, unpressured family event.

A CHILD-CENTERED DAY

The third change that will reverberate throughout your family life is your child's play—the activities that fill your child's day and the environment in which they take place. If you have chosen to be at home or to have in-home care for the first couple of years of your child's life, you certainly make that choice for your child's sake, but that doesn't mean that she is the sole, or even the central, focus of each day. You (or whoever replaces you) have a house to run. Shopping, laundry, cooking can be fascinating activities for a child, and sometimes that is your goal—checking where each item on your shopping list came from, for example, to see which is from farthest away (Dijon mustard, olive oil, soy sauce?); "helping" your child help you shred lettuce for salad or crumble bread for dressing; turning your toddler loose with the vacuum cleaner. But in the interests of efficiency, just as often you are probably concentrating on the job at hand, hoping your child will distract herself sufficiently not to get in the way.

In contrast, group care gears everything to the children.

In Chapter 1, we talked about the importance of mirrors and soft toys where toddlers could see them. For two-, three-, and four-year-olds, a child-sized world matters too. Get down on your hands and knees and crawl around your living room and kitchen. The spraddle of chair legs and walls of cabinet doors are your two-year-old's world. The pots and pans dragged out daily, the toys that frequently look like litter to parents provide the only color and pizzazz to a child. In a center, though, the pictures are at the *child*'s eye level. The furniture is her size. The toilets and sinks are designed with her size in mind, and electrical outlets are covered or out of reach.

The toys, too, are different. Sometimes it's a matter of more variety. You may have a half dozen puzzles; a day-care mother or a center has four or six or ten times that many. Yours are more apt to be cardboard, with fragile pieces easily lost or damaged; a center will have wood ones, easier for small hands to work with. You may have Lego and blocks, but you won't have as much, or as much space to lay it out. The painting easels will be bigger and more stable and always out; the range of paints (and the subsequent mess) will be greater than most parents can handle. You may have a swing set, but yours probably doesn't look like a castle, with tunnels and climbing nets. You may have a sandbox, but do you have a water table? If she wants to ride a tricycle at a center, she'll probably have several to choose from, along with a scooter and a wagon.

The environment and the toys are only part of the reason that a child's day is busier in group care. Her days have more structure as well. Centers make a conscious effort to alternate active and quiet activities throughout the day, but compared to a day spent at home amusing herself, a child at a center will be operating at fever pitch. Most child care centers try to get children outdoors twice each day, for example. Weather plays a role, of course, but even in very cold climates, on very cold days, the children will be outside for fifteen minutes, morning and afternoon. When the weather is really bad, the four- and five-year-olds, sometimes three-year-olds, who are in group care may go to a skating rink or to a mall where they can have a good long walk, with plenty of shop windows to keep them interested. But even inside, there may be marching to music; there may be tumbling; there may be indoor climbing areas.

The activities will probably not be confined to the center or day-care home. She will have trips to the library, to puppet shows, to a local television show to see behind the scenes, to the hospital during community helper preschool week. When she travels to and from these events, she may take routes that you don't in a van unlike your car. She begins to put together her own map of the world, which is not quite the same as yours. When you go to the park, for example, it's a different place than it used to be: Now she knows that Katy lives nearby.

Her world expands to include other people, too. She is watching or playing alongside of, or even beginning to play with, other children, all of whom entertain and stimulate and stretch her all day long. In a center, she now knows at least two teachers, the director, and the cook, and she may see other teachers on the playground. She knows the parents of other children. When children are tested for their reactions to "strange" situations, those who have been in child care handle them with much more poise than those who have not. Visit a center and you'll understand why. Children accept your presence without fear, even welcome you; a child is quite apt to come up to you and ask, "Are you Sam's mommy?"

Thus, at the end of the day, you're picking up a child who has had a saturated, absolutely child-oriented day. If she is at the stage when the focus of life is exploration, she has done that; if she is at

the stage when she plays alongside other children, watching intently, she has done that; if she is at the stage of beginning to share
and be part of a group, she has worked at that. Just as she has had
most of the food she needs—in other words, she has had all the
emphasis on child-development and stimulation that she needs.

What does this mean for you?

You may have thought of evening as the catch-up time, time to
squeeze in all the parenting and teaching and guiding and coaxing
you haven't been able to do all day. But she comes to you each
evening having had all the variety and action she needs. You are
free to concentrate on quieter times together: putting photographs
in an album, for example, or reading, or furnishing a dollhouse,
instead of big motor muscle play. Barbie and GI Joe are two
generations old now. Do you still have your own, with the outfits
and accessories of your childhood? Take a nostalgic trip together.

All the shifts child care makes in a child's habits—eating, sleeping, play—point you in the same direction. Your child is now
ready for quieter evenings, evenings that may seem longer both
because there's no big meal and because her bedtime is later. It's
true that you have very little choice about the shape of the evenings. But the trade-off, we think, is a golden one: You are no
longer single-handedly in charge of satisfying your child's every
need. As one mother said, "Quality time isn't only what you do,
it's what you haven't had to do." Now evenings and weekends can
be family-oriented rather than child-development–oriented. Long
walks with the dog, said one mother. More time spent with grandparents, said another. Talk with no intent to teach but just because
you're together. Preschoolers seem to love laundry: sorting dirty
clothes and folding clean ones. You can include counting and colors, just as when your child "helps" you in the kitchen you can
name vegetables. All this means more intimate and private and
contemplative times, as the family unwinds together. It may be a
more appealing routine for all of you.

ROLLING WITH THE PUNCHES:

Problems with a Small *p*

. . . .

There are bound to be points of friction in child care. Some are unique to one form—like whether (and how much) to allow a sitter to use the car—while other threads of tension seem to run through every kind of care. Even when you are sure of the rightness of your choice—both the form of child care and the person—you may well come up against these issues over and over again.

It's handy to know that ahead of time. For one thing, you'll know that such disagreements are not sufficient reason to scout around for a new caregiver—you'd almost certainly have the same problem the next time round as well. Then too, common frictions often stand in for quite different issues underneath; once you're aware of that, you can grapple with what's really bothering you. Finally, if you know ahead of time where possible problems lie, you can think them through and rehearse your strategies in advance.

We're going to discuss the common rubbing points of each kind of child care, and then show you how to set up a relationship with your caregiver in which talking over these kinds of minor conflicts can be done without damage and may even strengthen your relationship.

IN-HOME CARE:
Chores, Social Life, Privileges

There are two areas of disagreement common to in-home care, and a third common to in-home care outside of big cities, so if you and your housekeeper/nanny/sitter have frequent discussions about any of these, you're not alone. If you haven't, said one mother darkly, just wait. To which we would add, if you have thrashed them out thoroughly and think they are settled once and for all, just wait.

The prickliest and most constant bone of contention between sitters and their employers is television. If you have in-home care, you must accept the fact that television will be a central fact of your child's environment. The exceptions are too rare even to make a blip in the statistics. Television will be background noise, toy, entertainment, companion.

The fact that parents and caregivers routinely disagree on the use of television, though, doesn't mean that the issue is always the same. The reason may relate to the age—and therefore the needs—of your child, or it may have more to do with differences in the way you and your sitter picture her job.

If you have an infant who sleeps hours every day, you can't reasonably argue that the time your caregiver spends watching television during naps is being stolen from your child. That doesn't mean parents of infants like it. But the issue is not television's effect on your child, it is how to define the caregiver's duties and her free time. Is naptime free time? By using it as free time, is she neglecting other duties? Are you, in fact, saying that she ought to have other duties that weren't part of the original job definition?

A sitter's duties should have been spelled out carefully when you hired her, of course, but as new parents and/or new employers, you may have been ill prepared to do so. If you liked her, you wanted her and were afraid she'd go elsewhere; besides, you probably had no realistic idea of how much more laundry, errands, and overall mess there would be when you added a baby. Now that you do realize it, the rules are already in place—and you are stiff with resentment that she has time for hours of television daily while you don't even have time to get as much sleep as you need.

That's the framework for a dispute about television at the infant stage: it's really a renegotiation and discussion of what her job entails.

As your infant turns into a toddler, the role of television changes. In the world of a six-month-old, what equals in fascination that colorful, wonderfully noisy, ever-changing box? To her, it may seem better than a mirror—she'll learn her own routines after a time. It's *not* better than a loving adult. On the other hand, it may be more interesting to the nanny than your baby is, or she may genuinely feel that if she is watching "All My Children" while holding your baby on her lap, she's doing her job.

Television at this stage is a pricklier issue to discuss because by explaining what makes you unhappy you may seem to attack your sitter's tastes. Then again, once your infant has reached toddlerhood, television becomes easier to control without any discussion at all. Just plan a daily program that leaves no time for it: outdoor play, preferably twice a day; some kind of play group, whether it is with the child of a friend, a baby exercise group, or an infant swimming class. Books and puzzles set out in the morning, questions asked about them at night. Story-telling sessions at the library. Trips to the local firehouse, community helper preschool week at your neighborhood hospital, or just bus trips, planned to various parts of your town. Your paper lists events for children weekly; read it and plan around it.

Now, that's a lot of work. But if your caregiver is warm, if she loves your baby and you know your baby loves her, you may want to preserve that relationship despite the effort. The fact that she's warm and loving doesn't mean that she's inventive as well, nor does it mean that she will resent your planning for her. She may be diverted along with your child. If you have been afraid that you have forfeited too much parenting by not being at home, helping plan the days will also help to reassure you that you still have a critical role.

Your sitter may watch television for another reason. She may be lonely. And that brings us to the second most common problem area with in-home care: your caregiver's social life and how it affects your own and your child's. If your sitter has few friends, she may leave unless she finds some, and if you dislike her friends (and/or their charges), how will they influence your child's life?

If your sitter doesn't have friends, that automatically means that she is working outside her neighborhood, whether she comes to you from a state or country two thousand miles away or from a neighborhood three miles away. She may also be shy. Whatever the reason, if you want her to stay, you must help her find friends. If you don't, you'll lose her.

Sometimes you'll have support. Care for Kids, Inc., which places young women from the Midwest in the Connecticut area, assigns each one a big sister and plans several social events for them throughout the year. If you don't have that kind of support, you'll have to go exploring. You'll find that a sitter needs two sets of friends: other sitters to meet during the day for walks, play, sitting together at the neighborhood playground, and friends for when she is off-duty. (If she doesn't live in, obviously her off-duty friends are her own affair.) Many families have registered for baby exercise and swimming classes not for the baby's sake but for the sitter's. Some have registered with mothers' groups and even family counseling for the same reason. Walk around your neighborhood during a weekday, and you'll see two different clusters of strollers: mothers here, caregivers there. The groups rarely mix. Be sure your sitter knows where she'll meet others.

As she makes friends with other sitters, you need to meet them too. As necessary as friendships are, you don't want them to become so important that the nannies are inattentive to the children in their care. And you need to know the families for whom the other sitters work. Your child will play most often with the children your sitter's friends are caring for. You may think that's unimportant—and at six months perhaps it is—but by two-and-a-half or three, it will matter a great deal. Many sitters think their job means putting their child's needs first. Period. These children get no practice in sharing and no realistic idea of how groups work, nor do any of the children who play with them. Your own child's concept of friendship will be either that of a pitched battle or of catering to somebody else all the time. That's extreme. There may be lesser problems like lots of yelling and bathroom language or a child whose parents think in terms of name brands, so that your child either copies her or feels less worthy because she has no Polos.

For these reasons, some parents choose their sitter's friends as carefully as they chose her, arranging play dates, asking ahead about family policies on television and discipline. But you won't always be able to outwit this one.

To meet people when she's off the job, help your sitter look into adult education courses at your local high school, church groups for young adults, even bars where singles congregate. Some families have even bought their nannies health club memberships.

Ironically, if you are successful in adding people to your sitter's life, other problems then arise. For her off-the-job friends, you'll be forced to think through a new category of rules. Of course she can't drink on the job, but what if she lives with you and comes in having drunk too much? Do you have a right to set a curfew?

What if she wants to entertain somebody in her room? If she can't smoke while she's working, can she while she's entertaining somebody?

The third constant area of heated discussion is reserved for families outside big cities: the use of the car.

There are probably as many sets of rules regarding use of the car as there are families. Here's a rundown of questions you may face. Are you going to forbid all use of the car? You might begin that way, but you probably won't be able to stick to it. What about car pools to nursery school, grocery shopping, trips to the library or even to the emergency room? What about for her own use? Is she covered under your insurance? Who pays for the gas? Who pays for any damage to the car? On or off the job? If you need someone who drives and your favorite applicant doesn't have a license, do you pay for her driving lessons? If she wants to buy her own car, will you co-sign for the loan?

Television, social life, cars—these are issues without easy answers, and families are going to draw up many different sets of rules to cope with them. We advise you to check on the policies of other families in your neighborhood. If everyone you talk to is very restrictive in their use of the car, you may find it easier to be firm yourself. You may learn other families' trade secrets for limiting television. On the other hand, you may find that your own impulse is to be much stricter in every area. Unless you pay much more than your neighbors, you'll have trouble with that—your sitter will be hired out from under you.

In general, we find that no one is ever quite satisfied with the rules they work out. Caregivers universally feel that they should have a little more freedom than you think desirable; parents, on the other hand, always feel to some degree taken advantage of. If you all feel, perhaps grudgingly, that you have sacrificed about the same amount, you've probably reached the best possible balance.

FAMILY DAY CARE:
Questionable Friends, Activities, and Illnesses

Television is a continuing concern in family day care too. The advantage of a family day-care mother is that she can provide a warm, continuing presence in a home setting. The disadvantage is that her home doesn't have as many things to look at or play with as a center does, and a day-care mother, like a sitter, tends to take each day as it comes rather than having a program. Your child may spend a lot of the time in her crib or on her caregiver's lap in front of the television set. It may not be mindless television—it may be "Sesame Street" and "Electric Company," with all the children chanting along. But it is not a planned program that changes from hour to hour and day to day while your child interacts with others.

You may not object to that. If you do, you might make some of the same suggestions that you would to an in-home sitter about trips to the nearest firehouse or hospital, to the library for story hour, and check on the local events for children week to week in your paper. This time, though, you're dealing not with an employee but with somebody who runs a business. She may be grateful to you—we all get in ruts, and other people can point out to us things we haven't stumbled over ourselves. But she may be happy just as she is, and if you want to change your child's environment, you may have to move her to a new one.

The second source of difficulties in family day care relates to the range of ages of the children. In general, sitters who are friends take care of children in the same age range. In family day care, the children may range in age from a few months to kids who come to the home after school, and that poses other kinds of problems. Older kids tend to take over the play of younger ones. If two-year-olds are playing quite happily at a two-year-old level, a three-year-old, left out and bored, will try to change the play to something that more nearly suits *his* needs. Younger kids tend to imitate older ones, even when the age range is a big one and the imitation is inappropriate. In one case, a three-year-old's first song was "Virginity," from *Grease,* taught to her by the day-care mother's nine-year-old daughter.

Overall, these resemble sibling conflicts—which are difficult enough to handle when siblings have the same parents and the same house rules. In family day care, the rules are much more complicated. Suppose an unhappy four-year-old, jealous of his infant brother, is making life difficult not for the baby but for your toddler, eighteen months. If both were your children, you could be comfortable about working out a balance over the course of the day. A conscientious family day-care mother will try to keep an eye on the relationship, but your child may still spend her days trying to defend herself against somebody far more powerful, without you as a buffer.

If your child gets locked into a relationship you don't like, your choices are few. You can speak to the family day-care mother, but as we said, she can't drastically change the situation between any of her charges. You can move to another family day-care home, but problems that arise from differences in ages are part of this kind of child care.

You will also probably have problems with minor illnesses in a day-care home. Studies have shown that day-care mothers are generally more willing to accept a child who is unwell, particularly with upper respiratory infections, than a center is. That's a great relief if you're the parent of the child who is unwell, but what if you're not? What if one parent in the group consistently brings in a sniffly child, and as a result your family teeters from one cold to the next all winter long?

Finally—and all too common—are the problems caregivers have with parents: parents who are late, either in picking up their children or in paying—and frequently the culprits are the same.

Those parents who are consistently between ten and fifteen minutes late are more than likely also those who promise to pay the next morning after the evening payment is due.

CENTER-BASED CARE:
Locking Horns with the System

Some common problems between parents and child care centers are similar to those with sitters and day-care mothers, and some are unique to center-based care.

One of the problem areas, interestingly enough, is almost the flip side of too much television. As we've pointed out, sitters and day-care mothers often fall back on television for lack of other ideas of what to do. That probably won't happen in a child care center; because a center cares for many more children, the days are more likely to be carefully planned ahead of time. To you, the parent, that may well be a plus, but it too will lead to tension because there are going to be times when your child's wants won't fit into the day's plans. A sitter's job is to respond to what your daughter wants; a day-care mother, too, can drop plans or pick them up according to children's moods. A center is less likely to bend.

Sometimes the friction is over a day-by-day activity. Your child may come home whimpering, "Miss Mary never lets me paint." That sounds like trouble between your daughter and Miss Mary. However, it's more likely to mean that Tuesday isn't the day to paint, that on this particular day the class was divided into two groups and she was in the nonpainting group, or that she was arguing with the other child at the double easel and was tempted away to the water table.

Sometimes children and center policies conflict. Many toddlers actively dislike wearing shoes, for example. At home, with one-to-one care and less outdoor play, that may cause few problems. A

center, legally responsible for the children's health, and well aware
of stones, splinters, and fire ants, can't allow children to go bare-
foot—or without socks or jackets or whatever a child has decided
to leave in her cubby that day. But you can be sure that a child
will tearfully greet parents with some version of "The devil made
me do it," to explain the lost clothing at the end of the day.
Another common difficulty is the child who wants to bring a
favorite toy. It may make a Show and Tell appearance, but it will
then stay in her cubby till she goes home.

Such encounters are inevitable—in fact, the only time you
should worry is if they don't happen. One mother heard alarm
bells go off when a center director said her daughter "marched to a
different drummer"; she feared, rightly, that the child was being
allowed to operate like a loose cannon among the other children,
and she moved her to a center where she was gently but firmly
treated as part of the group. The tearful interpretation a child puts
on any kind of difference of opinion is inevitable too. Children
think in terms of high-stakes drama, not subtleties.

The second area of problems occurs when parents fail to follow
through. All parents agree that field trips are terrific, for example,
but a few inevitably forget about the notices requesting money for
skate rental, only to be upset when their child cannot skate. Parents
may forget to send in the extra clothes every child needs, or they
may plan a business trip without telling the center when they'll be
away and who will pick up their child.

And parents, like children, come up against a center's policies.
There is a lot of friction about minor illnesses. A center's teachers
often may not give medicine and they will not administer oint-
ments to the genital area unless medically prescribed—both common requests. A parent comes in with a sniffling child, saying,
"She's not feeling too well. I don't want her to go outside." A
nanny or babysitter will respond to that, and a day-care mother
may, but a teacher in a center is responsible for many children; she
can't give that kind of individual attention to a single one.

There may be differences about discipline. "Esmeralda hit Susie yesterday, and I just told her to hit right back if it happens again" may make emotional sense, but it will not be permitted. Corporal punishment (which includes spanking, another common request) is not permitted in most licensed centers. The contract that parents sign spells out the center's policies, but many fail to read it or perhaps forget about a rule until they're affected by it.

Parents with children in centers have problems with payment and lateness too, undoubtedly for the same reasons as other kinds of child care. But parents have less room to maneuver because, unlike sitters or day-care mothers, most centers have systems firmly in place to handle such problems. There will be fines for lateness, and frequently half-tuition is required to hold a child's place when she is ill for an extended period of time. And these things too are in the contract.

HOW TO KEEP A GOOD THING GOING

As we've described these incidents they seem so minor as to be silly, too foolish to discuss. Imagine the dialogue. ("If you know about Eden and Cruz's wedding, you must have been watching 'Santa Barbara.'" "What's this about Miss Mary not letting my kid paint?") But caregivers know, and you'll soon discover, that incidents pile up, and anger piles up along with them. Then it can be too late to do anything, and you may be forced to move on to somebody or somewhere else.

It's a big effort to find good child care. It makes more sense to use your energy making this relationship work than looking around, particularly when problems will arise in a new situation too.

As we've tried to show, underlying all the problems we've described are a few basic difficulties, all of which can be handled within the bounds of your present child care if it's basically good.

The first is the matter of your fulfilling your obligations. This covers everything from attempting to add tasks to a sitter's job beyond those you discussed when you hired her, to being consistently late to pick up your child at a day-care home, to not checking the bulletin board at the center to see if you must send in a smock or egg cartons or skate-rental money.

This sounds easy to solve, doesn't it? Then why is it such a common problem?

Psychologists have one answer. Late parents may unconsciously be trying to prove that the caregiver relationship is a caring one with the flexibility of friendship rather than a businesslike arrangement of rules and fees. It would be warmer and more reassuring.

Lateness in paying and in picking up may frequently have a simpler explanation, though—the cramped and busy lives of parents. Working people don't always have control over their time. A meeting runs late, a boss's meeting runs late, the line at the bank was too long to cash a check during a lunch hour—we are all sliding for bases too much of the time. Things slip, and sometimes those things relate to child care.

If you have problems with lateness, you *must* change because every caregiver in every kind of care will resent it. Forgive yourself for whatever has gotten in your way—but find ways to avoid it in the future. If you want to think of your caregiver as a friend, good for you. A warm, caring relationship is a goal we applaud, but stretching the rules is not the way to achieve it. Friends treat one another fairly, rather than taking advantage. Instead, make a conscious effort to demonstrate the caring in positive ways, like remembering your caregiver's birthday or praising something new she is doing with the children. Is there a holiday poster on the front door? Comment on it.

If your lateness is a function of too little time, experiment till you find something that works better. Try having your spouse pick up your child for a while. You may have to ask a neighbor to take on the task of picking up your child in return for some favor on your part. If the problem is late payment, set rigorous goals for yourself. Plan to cash your check two days ahead of time instead of one. Get a cash card—whatever it takes. It would be a shame to spoil a relationship that works for a reason wholly within your control.

A second set of problems directly concerns your child, like Lucinda's not being allowed to paint. We've described what may really be happening in such instances, so you know that this is not a painting problem; it's a communications problem.

The first step to open the channels is to remind yourself of something we said in Chapter 5: You are not going to get perfection day in and day out. And a relationship without conflict is not perfect; it's artificial. Like a fragile vase, one crack and it falls to pieces. The relationship that lasts is the one in which you learn to deal with conflicts as they arise and are satisfied with the results, even though they may not be what you imagined.

How does this come about?

Begin before there are problems, in the honeymoon period. Whenever there's something remotely positive to say, say it. Tell the sitter how fresh and sweet-smelling your daughter is when you hug her at the end of the day. Comment on the children's art at the center or on how skilled the children are at getting their boots on and off. Will you feel self-conscious? Perhaps, but this is the stuff of your caregiver's day. You know as well as she does the effort such things represent.

Such comments give her important feedback; just as important, they are opportunities for miniconversations. Now, if the caregiver has something to mention to you, she has the opportunity to do so. If not, you are simply establishing a framework for frequent talk.

Let us repeat the word *frequent*. We advise setting a regular weekly time to talk to your sitter. It's for the purposes of exchanging information: we're running low on Pampers; she's almost outgrown her stretch suits; she's chewing on her fists a lot—do you think she's ready for solid food? But it also establishes a comfortable conversational relationship between you. Then when the discussion must also include tough issues like television or playmates, the setting, at least, is a familiar one.

At either a day-care home or a center, you remember, we recommended taking fifteen minutes at pickup time. This is the time to chat, to praise or to deal with minor complaints. It's best not to telephone ahead of time, ask to speak to her privately, or even to sit down. The morning after Lucinda informed you she wasn't allowed to paint, walk her to her room and on the way back catch the director and say something like, "I understand there was a shortage of fingerpaints yesterday." If the director looks blank and says she'll get back to you, you can already be assured that the incident is minor or she'd be aware of it. But she probably knows about it. She'll give one of the explanations we mentioned above, or she may welcome the opportunity to say, "You know, Lucinda is a beautiful painter, but she has some trouble sharing the paints."

Now, that sounds like a minor comment—and it is, or the director would have called and asked you for a conference. But it will probably make your heart drop to your shoes just the same. Criticism of our children, however mild, is devastating. They are a part of ourselves. It's as though someone had just said casually, "You know, your left arm is much bigger than your right; does it cause you any problems?" For working parents criticism is even more damning because on some level we count on our children to be perfect to reassure ourselves that we are doing the right thing by them. You might know very well that Lucinda is slow to share, but to be told so by an outsider can be painful.

But your child's growth will always be expressed in incidents like this—demonstrations of what she has not quite mastered. Since much of her growth will take place in child care, this isn't the last time you'll hear a pointed comment. It may not even be the last time this week. Talking about such things and sharing them *must* be part of your child care relationship. You have tried to build a bond by positive comments; when you hear a negative one, you'll know both how far you've come and how far you have to go.

The only way to accept such a comment is to accept as well that you and your caregiver are on the same side. She is *not* an outsider, though in the beginning you may have to grit your teeth to say so. You are both members of your child's family. So, teeth gritted, respond to her comment with, "Anything we should be doing differently at home?" And the center director will take a minute to explain how, when Lucinda got piggy over the paints, the teacher distracted her with the water table. So, next time Lucinda screams, "Mine! Mine!" at home, you now know to ignore her comment and redirect her attention to something else. And instead of a small, festering worry, you've learned something.

The third area of differences concerns policies, the underlying rules that define your sitter's job or a day-care home or a child care center. Policies are generally not easily changed.

Because you're the employer, you can change the definitions of a sitter's job; on the other hand, because good sitters are highly sought after, she may leave. Free time and duties other than child care are concerns that will be with you as long as you have in-home care, so take the time to think about how you really feel before you discuss them. Be honest about the enormous strains of a two-job family and about what chores somebody else could do to lighten your load. Be honest with yourself too about what behaviors are and are not acceptable, and be sure that your caregiver knows how you feel. Will even a small amount of regular television watching eventually erode your relationship? Truly? Then she deserves to know. If the risk of co-signing a car loan won't undermine your relationship, fine, but if it will, don't do it, even if you risk losing her. If you don't want your child playing with the child your sitter's best friend takes care of, do you feel so strongly about it that her job is at risk? You must make that plain. Not bluster, but a clear spelling out of your priorities, first to yourself, and then to her.

You'll be most successful if you can put the discussion in the context of your child's changing needs. As your child grows, her needs change constantly. It's the truth (which is always handy), but it is also a way of bringing up the need for change in an uncritical way. What you worked out laboriously a few months—or even weeks—ago may not be appropriate any longer. With luck, you framed your original definition of the job in this context, but if not, make that the context now.

It's a good idea to combine it with a salary adjustment if you can. Explain that it is a one-time adjustment because her job is being put on a different footing from when she was hired, that her job is bound to change again as your child's needs do, but that's now part of the job definition and her salary won't necessarily change next time. This is a must discussion because you will need to refer to changing needs, and thus changes in her job, many more times in the future.

Look at the issues from her side too. If both parents work normal days, a sitter's day will be that long plus your morning and evening commutes. She must have some free time during those hours, just as you would yourself. If you don't acknowledge that, she will either leave or find ways to take time anyway while feeling guilty.

If this sounds as though we are overly sympathetic to the sitter's feelings, it's because we know that you need to be. Your sitter is dependent on you for her job. Criticism, always hard to take, is doubly difficult when a person is dependent. Many people wilt under it; even those who perform adequately may become grudging. And that won't do. If this relationship is to succeed, you *must* feel that your caregiver is happy with your baby each day, or your baby will be the one to suffer. So be protective of your sitter's dignity throughout any discussion.

A talk with a day-care mother must be handled a bit differently because your objectives are different. Conflicts between children of different ages, constant minor illnesses, television-based amusement are as integral a part of most day-care homes as a contract is of a center. You can ventilate your feelings, but you cannot realistically expect much change. The best choice may be to change the mix— to add a few afternoons at a center. This will enable you to keep the day-care mother's warm presence in your child's life and to enable your child to participate in planned activities with children her own age.

If you object to a child care center's policies, you will probably not have much power to change them. But talking about them is still essential. Suppose naps are a problem, for example, because your daughter has begun staying up till ten. Learning that centers must follow state regulations for rest periods won't make your evenings any easier, but it may take away your resentment. The center may have suggestions to ease your evening routine (we have some, too; see Chapter 14, page 198), like settling Lucinda with a book even though she's not sleepy.

As with Lucinda's painting, in other words, you are more apt to find a way to live more happily with child care's methods than you are to change them. And that really is what you and your caregiver and your child learn through these day-to-day differences: how to live more happily with one another. An extended family—which is what we consider good child care to be—is not a fuzzy ideal. It never was. When the extended family of two generations ago worked well, it was because of the common sense and cooperation and commitment of all concerned. That's a sound model for successful child care today.

ONCE-IN-A-WHILE CARE

· ·

We can all identify with the scene in *Baby Boom* in which Diane Keaton, wild-eyed, tries to focus on an important business lunch while balancing a wriggling infant and finally checks the baby like a coat. We laugh with relief because—thank God!—it is happening to somebody else.

For once.

All of us have been there: sometime, often with little warning, every parent has needed temporary child care. You may have a special short-term need—your husband's bookkeeper is in the hospital and you have the accounting skills he desperately needs for the next few weeks. You may be job hunting. You may be moving. You may have a business trip scheduled and want to bring your child with you. Your children have a school holiday and you can't afford to take a vacation day to care for them. You may be divorced and have custody of your toddler for the next three weeks.

Maybe your child has chicken pox and you can't stay home with him.

We call this *once-in-a-while care*. That term covers many different needs, each with its own requirements and solutions. A few guidelines, however, apply to all of them.

- Expect to pay quite a bit more than you would for a regular sitter or center.

- Check out any sitter's health records as thoroughly as you would somebody you hired for long-term care. It's tempting to think that for a brief time it isn't as important. But tuberculosis is on the rise in this country; communicable diseases, drug use, and drunkenness are as threatening in a single afternoon as they are day in and day out. Ask the date of a person's last physical checkup. Yes, you'll feel awkward. Do it anyway.

- Since everybody will have emergencies sooner or later, even if you are completely content with your present child care provider, research a few names. Use them for Saturday night sitters now and then so that if and when something comes up, you are leaving your child with somebody you both know and trust.

- Finally, be sure that an impromptu solution is fair to all concerned. There seem to be news stories every week about children who accompany their fathers to work on school holidays, of a baby sleeping in a file drawer in Mommy's law office. It sounds cute. In real life it often means that the executive, feeling virtuous, hands the child over to a secretary, and the secretary is forced to become a caregiver without ever being asked.

Let's take each kind of once-in-a-while care and talk about what kind of coverage you need, who can best provide it, and how to find her.

ONE-TIME CARE

You are going to a funeral or a wedding, you have a job interview, or you have a business meeting and your husband's out of town.

What we are really talking about here is babysitting, except that since neither parent can be interrupted in case of emergency, you need somebody a bit more responsible than the fourteen-year-old next door. Your caregiver must be able to drive, probably to prepare food (and clean up afterward), and must know what to do in an emergency.

If you live in a small town, word of mouth may quickly provide you with names. Ask friends—somebody's parents may make a practice of helping in just such emergencies. Ask your friends' sitters for names. Your minister or rabbi or priest will know women in the congregation who might help out in this way.

If you live in a large city, you may not have these informal sources, but you have others. Look up the groups for retired people (Golden Age, Retired Citizens). Schools of nursing and colleges or universities are also good sources. (The school's Student Employment Bureau will either handle your request or tell you where to go.)

PART-TIME CARE

There are two very different part-time needs: "regular" once-in-a-while care, to cover something like working three mornings a week, and "unpredictable" part-time care, for a doctor's appointment every other week or occasional volunteer work or substitute teaching.

If you need regular part-time care, children and child care will both adapt quite well. Day-care mothers are not very interested in part-time children unless they can charge their full weekly fee. It's appealing work for many sitters, though—probably for the same reason that part-time work appeals to the parents. Students may be able to schedule their courses around a small but regular sitting job. Child care centers find that a child who comes on a systematic part-time basis does very well. Your part-time child will have to be registered (which requires immunization records and a one-time fee of $15–$35; their paperwork is the same as if he were going to attend full-time).

On the other hand, if, like a substitute teacher, you need child care frequently but on an irregular and perhaps last-minute basis, this sporadic kind of care is often the most difficult to find. You'd like to have a regular sitter, yet you aren't providing enough work to keep her busy; you can't even guarantee her a specific day each week. Your child feels shaken out of his routine each time. Apparently a child's internal clock adapts to a weekly Tuesday routine better than to one of Tuesday this week, Thursday next week, and nothing the week after that. Thus, he's probably always on his worst behavior—normal, perhaps, but it hardly makes sitters want to bend over backward for you.

You'll need to develop a long list of sitters to increase your chances of finding one free to come. A center will take children on this unpredictable basis if there is room, but they won't hold a regular space for you. Center or sitters, it's a good idea to use their services now and then even when you don't need them. You want the setting to remain familiar to your child so that whenever he goes there he is returning to something he knows instead of making a whiny adjustment over and over again.

FULL-TIME CARE FOR A BRIEF PERIOD

You work for a temporary agency for two- and three-week periods, then you are home again. You are looking for permanent child care and need somebody to tide you over. You have custody of your child for the next two weeks—or three months. Your sitter or day-care mother just called to say that she has relatives visiting and won't be working for the next week or so (unhappily all too common).

The sitter to whom you turn for one-time or part-time care can sometimes step in for a few full-time weeks, so begin with your babysitting sources. Sometimes, of course, a sitter can't be tied down in this way—if she works part-time for two or three people, she can't give up her other clients for a few weeks.

Child care centers will definitely register a child on this temporary basis if they have room. If you want in-home care, though, and your regular sitters can't help you, there are three further possibilities: babysitting services, sitting services, and temporary agencies.

A babysitting service is just what it sounds like: groups of sitters registered through an agency. The agency may know little about them besides their name or it may check them out thoroughly, including a medical record. Babysitting services are listed in the Yellow Pages. Check with the Chamber of Commerce to see if they endorse or recommend a particular service.

A sitting service sounds like the same thing but is in fact quite different; it is more like a temporary agency for medical personnel. Because of rising medical costs and the shrinking population of nurses, many hospitals rely on sitters—licensed practical nurses or nurses' aides—to stay with patients who need to be observed but don't need the full-time care of a nurse. Hospitals may have their own sitter services or they may endorse one in the community.

People who work for these services don't always work with children. (Then again, others seek out cases with children as a way of rejuvenating themselves after working with serious illnesses.) They're also expensive—probably twice the cost of a regular sitter. But they are much more highly trained and you may feel much more comfortable about their ability to handle emergencies. This is an especially good source in the summer, when fewer people are ill and an agency needs to keep its people employed or lose some of them.

You may be able to reach a hospital sitting service directly through its switchboard, or you may be referred to a sitting service. They are also listed in the Yellow Pages; if you look there, be sure to cross-check through nearby hospitals or the Chamber of Commerce to see if they are recommended.

Some communities may also have temporary agencies (Upjohn is one) that specialize in medical positions. Chances are that they carry practical nurses, nurses' aides, even nursing students on their books. They will charge about the same as the sitting services; check them out in the same way.

If you know beforehand that you'll need temporary full-time care, try to get the caregiver into your home once or twice ahead of time, despite the expense, so that she will be less strange to your child. Spell out your daily routine carefully: the route the car pool takes, how he likes his tuna fish sandwich, favorite books, and videotapes. As long as *his* day stays the same and he knows you'll be home within hours, he'll be fairly comfortable.

ROUND THE CLOCK FOR A BRIEF PERIOD

You're a flight attendant and are gone for two to three days at a clip, then home for a week. Your job requires that you travel frequently. Your husband has a convention and you want to go with him. You plan a vacation without your child.

One thing you must discuss with anyone you hire is her feelings about a mother or parents who travel without children. There are people to whom you will be a "bad" mother for letting your job take you away from your child; there are some to whom vacationing parents are selfish parents. That will be reflected in the care your child gets; he'll become "you poor little thing." Since he'll feel insecure anyway, he doesn't need that added threat.

If you have a housekeeper who lives in, theoretically travel should not be a problem. But taking her care for granted in this situation is the kind of abuse that can stretch your relationship to the breaking point and beyond. Discuss the trip beforehand, ask if it is possible for her, and say that since she will be taking on added responsibility, you will pay her accordingly.

Any of the sitters you find by word of mouth may be willing to stay round the clock for brief periods. On the other hand, the added responsibility may make you turn to the more highly trained people of a sitter service or a temporary agency. Retired couples frequently do this for people they know—their children and friends of their children.

If you have regular child care and need extra help only in the evenings or over a weekend, frequently the teacher at a child care center will help out. As we have said elsewhere, centers don't encourage it because either child or teacher may begin to think of the relationship as special during class hours as well. But it's still common, and you will feel comfortable that the person is honest and knows your child.

When you will be out of town while the sitter is there, your responsibilities don't end with finding a suitable sitter. For whoever comes, you must provide very specific written instructions. It can be helpful to write a narrative, day by day, of what to do and not to do, from the way you like mealtimes to go, to the playmates who are most successful, to television rules. You might ask your child to help you put together a travel booklet of photographs of the things he thinks you'll miss most while you're away, and then offer to make a similar booklet for him of what he'll miss most while you're gone.

Put together a list of emergency names. It should include at least one friend in the neighborhood, a relative, if one lives nearby, and your pediatrician's name. At the same time, tell your pediatrician that you will be away and for how long, and give him the name of your sitter. Ask the friend and/or relative to stop by each night. Your children need to see a familiar face; for both children and caregiver, it will give the feeling of continuing with the same routine. Plan to call each night at roughly the same hour.

CHILD CARE ON THE ROAD

You've been sent to Denver for the week and you want to take your toddler. The whole family has been invited to accompany your husband to his convention. You plan a skiing vacation and you want to include your two-year-old. The whole family will be traveling to a wedding three hundred miles away, but your child won't be attending the service or reception.

If you are taking your child with you on a business trip, *never* rely on the secretaries at the company you visit to "amuse" him. What will you do instead?

Even if your child is in child care at home, child care on the road is a very different matter. By the time you reach your destination, your child has already spent hours in a car or in a train or plane, which is strange to him. He will be spending his days in a strange place, sleeping in an unfamiliar bed, with none of his regular playmates around. When *you* leave him, his last connection to the known world is gone. Deep down he knows *(knows)* that you are never coming back. Small wonder that his face is solemn and his eyes enormous. Contrast his inner nightmare with your own desire on a vacation to relax and feel a freedom you don't feel at home, and you can see the possible pitfalls.

Your child is not going to have as good a time as you do, so don't expect him to. But you can minimize some of his fears. Explain what will be happening ahead of time: "We're going to Disney World. Sometimes we'll be going on rides, but sometimes Mommy and Daddy will go out to dinner or play tennis by themselves." Or "Cousin Ted is getting married, and we'll all be going to stay at Grandma's house, but Saturday afternoon somebody else will be coming there to stay with you."

Don't expect him to have a child care experience equal to whatever he has at home. If he's at a center, whether in a ski resort or at Walt Disney World, he is with a group of children strange not only to him but to the caregivers. The age range is undoubtedly wider than in his neighborhood center. The chances that the children have all come provided with immunization records are slim. The staff cannot set up a formal program. They are caring for children, but it is not formal, structured child care.

In some settings, like ski resorts, parents automatically pop their kids into the area's center—even those parents who don't use a child care center back home. But think through putting your child in group care when you are on vacation. Whenever he's away from home, your child is exposed to a number of germs for which he has no immunities. If he spends his days with children from many parts of the country, every one of them has come equipped with a separate family of germs. Your child is under stress as well. What are his chances of coming through this vacation without catching a cold? What kind of memories will he have? And what frame of mind will he be in when you begin to talking about the next vacation? Almost without exception, resorts can also provide you with a list of babysitters, a solution we prefer for preschoolers.

If your children are school-age or above, it's a different matter. Many hotels and resorts have junior programs—what amounts to a mini-camp—and children and parents tend to be mutually pleased with the arrangements.

When you need a sitter away from home, line up your care

ahead of time. The housekeeping department of the hotel is usually the place to begin. (At Walt Disney World Resort Hotels, for example, Kinder-Care provides in-the-room sitter service.) A hotel may endorse a sitter service, or the local Chamber of Commerce may do so. If they have no suggestions, ask them to look through the Yellow Pages for you. It's extremely important that you work through a service that is endorsed or underwritten or accountable to a source you trust, whether that's the hotel, a local hospital, or a Chamber of Commerce. If you're calling a service blind, ask for a business license, proof of insurance, and references—and pursue them. Make arrangements ahead of time, and verify them after you arrive.

Think too about the prerogatives you want your sitter to have. Most hotels have a swimming pool; will she be allowed to take your child there? (Does she have a lifesaving certificate? Does the hotel have a policy?) If there are other forms of recreation like sailing or rides, is she allowed to go on them with your child? What are you comfortable with? We are very conservative: We think the limits should be narrow and sharply defined. Plan to do the swimming and amusement park activities with your child yourself. Then if he falls off the merry-go-round in a strange place, at least *you're* there.

CARE IN TIME OF ILLNESS

Parents live in dread of illness—theirs, their caregiver's, their child's. Schedules that have been fitted together with such care suddenly crash like a house of cards. Centers and day-care mothers will warn you when you begin that you need to prepare for this kind of emergency care, and they mean it.

When your child is too sick to be in child care, you are looking for care for a sick child. That sounds repetitive, but think for a moment about what it means. When you're traveling, your child may be frightened but he's on his feet and at the top of his form. A sick child, though, needs his parents in ways that have nothing to do with nursing ability. If you keep a child home for a day, even two, when you see that he's on the threshold of an illness, you aren't talking about a huge amount of time. Forty-eight hours is one day home per parent. An increasing number of companies allow parents to use their own sick days to care for sick children, and we wish every company in this country would adopt the policy starting tomorrow morning. By now you know that we wouldn't lightly recommend that you stay home, so you know, too, how important we think your care is to your sick child.

There are exceptions, but not many. In these days of vaccines, chicken pox is almost the only childhood disease left—a phenomenon that probably has as much to do with two-job families as changes in the workplace. If you tried unsuccessfully to ease your child past an illness and he now has bronchitis, you can't stay home for the week to ten days that may be required. And flu, alas, is flu —although in that case, the whole family may be sick together. But whatever the situation is, bear in mind that in times of illness anybody else is a poor substitute for you.

What are the implications of that? First of all, it's important that a caregiver in times of illness be somebody the child knows. A grandmother or close family member is a clear first choice. If you have to rely on a sitter, she should be familiar and well liked, and that means, yet again, that you must be well prepared for an emergency ahead of time.

Make sure that child and caregiver know one another ahead of time. A list of two or three names is better than one, and at least one person on the list must have had chicken pox—if she hasn't, she may catch the virus in the form of shingles, and even grandmothers won't risk that. When you have a few names, use them in turn as evening sitters so that your child is comfortable with all of them.

The second requirement of a sitter for a sick child is that she be familiar with illness. When a child has chicken pox, you want a sitter who knows how uncomfortable he is and who is prepared to give him a soothing bath every hour if necessary. As in other situations where you need superresponsible care, you can turn to a sitter service or temporary health care agency.

Depending on where you live, you may have a second alternative. A new development in child care is caregivers who specialize in sick care. There are a few centers (Chicken Soup in Minneapolis is one). Occasionally, companies have a nurse on the payroll exclusively to care for the sick children of employees and thus cut down on working parents' expensive lost time.

Specialized sick-child care sounds very appealing, but there are arguments against it as well. Parents must consider that a center will always be a more stimulating setting than a home; how wise is that for a sick child? Will he get sicker and stay sick longer? The cost is usually about three times that of regular child care, which may make it impossible for all but the very few.

If it interests you, check with your local Chamber of Commerce, Y.M.C.A. or Y.W.C.A., a resource and referral agency, and your local day-care licensing service for centers or sitters that specialize.

NO ADVANCE WARNING

Your sitter is ill. A wire on your child's braces popped and he needs to get to the orthodontist immediately.

Although these are not drop-dead emergencies, the lack of advance warning can cause real anxiety.

If you have a housekeeper or nanny who lives in, a cold that might keep her from going to work won't keep her from caring for your child—who will almost certainly get her cold anyway. (That added dependability is the reason most frequently given for live-in care.) A day-care mother may have a substitute in case of illness, particularly if she works through an agency. Sometimes, too, the agency will help you out if she's ill for more than a day or two.

The person most apt to let you down is a sitter—either someone who comes to you by the day or who cares for two or three children in her home. She is also likely to give you little warning: The phone will ring at eight o'clock, or she may even tell you when you show up to drop your child off.

In this kind of emergency, you don't need the super-skilled care you would if your child was ill. On the other hand, you need somebody with a quality that may be even more rare: She must be able to come with little or no warning. This is the person (people) whose name will go on forms throughout your child's school years as your "designated back-up person." Nearby relatives and neighbors with children the same age, even if they don't regularly take care of children, are top choices here. Give her name and telephone number to the center or day-care mother as a person allowed to pick up your child; explain to your neighbor what you have done and that she will be asked to identify herself if called upon.

Whether or not money changes hands, you are essentially asking a favor of your friend. If you want this to work, be prepared to return the favor in some way and say so upfront.

Sooner or later, you'll probably have to make use of every kind of care we've described. It will never be fun—an emergency never is—but at least now you know that emergencies too can be handled.

SHARING THE TOUGH STUFF OF CHILDHOOD

There has been a lot of talk about the sadness parents feel when they miss a milestone. Here, we are looking not at *your* feelings, but at the effects on your child of your not being present as your child grows. Will your caregiver handle these milestones differently than you would? What influence do you have and how do you use it? Will a child's growth inevitably be different if she is always one of many children? How do you work with your child care provider so that each growth step is handled in the best way for your child? And if you work at cross-purposes, what is the effect on your child?

These are make-or-break issues for child care. We are talking about parenting styles and about how you can raise your child according to your personal beliefs even when you're not there all day. We're going to look at major growth steps for

. . . .

each age. We'll also discuss the crises that can happen at any age —moving, divorce, remarriage, death, serious illness, questions about religion. We'll look at how relationships—friendship, being an only child or a sibling—are affected by child care.

We are not going to spell out rigid rules of what kids should do when. You don't need help in following somebody else's opinions here; you need help in defining your own. Your first opinions might not always be your final ones—you can profit from your caregiver's experience, just as she can learn from what you strongly value. You may both change.

Remember, though, that you are still the parent. You *must* feel comfortable with the way your caregiver handles these issues or you've got to find something that works better. How can you tell when you've reached your personal breaking point —when your caregiver or child care are no longer meeting your child's—or your—needs? We'll talk about that too.

MASTERING THE UNIVERSE:

The First Two Years

. . . .

The first determined roll from tummy to back that changes his landscape forever, the first time he pulls himself up to stand with a gorgeous, ear-to-ear grin of triumph (only to break down in tears moments later when he realizes he has no idea how to sit down again), the first burbled syllables that can be optimistically interpreted as a word—these are what most parents imagine as the milestones of a baby's life. The idea of missing one of them is hard to bear.

Your caregiver can help: Ask her to call you the first time your son succeeds in drinking from a cup or creeps or crawls or pulls himself up to stand. A sensitive caregiver may go even further— one center director instructs her teachers never to tell parents a first has taken place. Instead they will say something like, "He was scooting around so fast today, I think he's about ready to take off and walk," or "He really chomped down on my finger today—I think that tooth is about to come through."

That director knows what you will discover: Infants make many strikes at these accomplishments. There are lots of teeter-totter steps, many funny rolling attempts to sit up. We sometimes think they are built up as "firsts" just to hit mothers over the head with guilt for working and not being on the spot when they happen. We don't mean to diminish your sense of loss—as men have known for years, it's wrenching to learn about progress second-hand. But our advice is, don't feel guilty for missing this kind of milestone. You will share a satisfying number of the attempts along the way.

What we fear is that in concentrating on these missed milestones, parents won't pay enough attention to events that are far more significant in these years, namely, the development of their own style of parenting, and learning to live with some of the common stresses in a parent/caregiver relationship. And that's what we're going to talk about in this chapter.

HOW PARENTS PICTURE THEIR BABY'S LIFE

Parents dismiss most of their child's early life as routine. You may ask your caregiver to keep a record of the amount your baby eats, for example, so that you know how much to feed him at home. She may warn you that you are almost out of disposable diapers. The day-care mother may give you advice on convincing a reluctant baby to sleep through the night.

Caregivers know that these daily exchanges are more important over the long run than when a baby sits or walks or talks because of what they reveal about the parents. Parents show their style— the kind of parents they are going to be—from their very first requests in the very first days of child care. When they look at the cribs, for example, some parents check the firmness of the mattress and how often each crib is cleaned while others want to be sure there's an overhead mobile or mirror. Some parents want their babies held a lot, others want their babies talked to a lot, still others (though not enough, say caregivers) ask how much time their babies are spending outdoors. Some parents want their babies fed on schedule and others on demand; some want their babies to "cry it out" and others never ever want that to happen.

You can see how a pattern of instructions reflects a parent's picture of babyhood. For example, some parents clearly think of holding almost as they do food. They imagine that an infant, replete with this physical expression of love, will happily set off on his daily round. Others picture their baby finding within himself the comfort he needs and finding satisfaction through what he can do for himself—a picture either more stern or more adventurous, depending on your point of view.

Caregivers will follow a parent's wishes to the extent that they can. A sitter caring for several children or a teacher at a center can't always let a baby cry himself to sleep, for example, because crying spreads from infant to infant like a juicy bit of gossip. But if you don't want your son held too much during waking hours, a caregiver will try to amuse or distract him into stopping his tears instead of picking him up. If you want him on a firm schedule, she will try to stretch his hours—again, within limits that don't unduly disturb other children and are reasonably fair to the baby.

We're not attempting to endorse one style of parenting over another—there's a case to be made for each—merely to say that it is important to become aware of your own style in these early months rather than backing into it without realizing what you've done. If you think that sounds improbable, believe us, it isn't. Caregivers agree that parents aren't often aware of the implications of what they are doing. They see their instructions less as choices than as "what everybody does"—a loose amalgam of what they have read, what most of their friends do, or what their mothers and grandmothers did.

Don't let that happen. Take advantage of the fringe benefits of child care—the experience of the caregiver and the chance to watch other children and parents. Try to find time to observe your child's group to see how different children operate; allow time to talk to other parents at pick-up time. Is your child frequently clutching at a caregiver's knees, for example, because you've asked that he not be held too much? Do the infants who are held more frequently seem more content? You don't have to do things the way that your parents did or the way that you've read about. These early months are a boon because cause and effect have such clear links. If you switch from scheduled feedings to feedings on demand, for example, you'll see some kind of change within a day or two. Ask your caregiver's opinion. Experiment. Your baby came with his own set of likes and dislikes. This is the time to set up the most important routine of all—working out the balance between what seems to make him happiest and what makes you feel most comfortable.

Before many months have passed, you'll realize why this effort is so important. As your infant turns into a toddler, he'll hit milestones on which you and your caregiver need to cooperate to do the best job for your child. Should he creep before he crawls? Use a walker? When should he give up his bottle? his pacifier? his blanket? And what if he bites? It will be easier to discuss them if you've already established a pattern of cooperation.

Instead of trying to describe every possible issue in these early years, we're going to talk about two—biting and toilet training. We've picked them for several reasons. They are among the most difficult issues for parents. Both assume different forms in child care than with parents at home (biting is more complicated, toilet training simpler). Biting involves learning *not* to do something socially *un*acceptable, while toilet training involves mastery— learning to *do* something socially *acceptable*. Between them, they represent the range of issues you and your caregiver will be working on and show the common stresses of any parent/caregiver relationship.

BITING:
The Toughest Issue in Child Care

You may be anxious about whether your infant sits and walks and talks at the right time, but biting will almost certainly be the first issue that makes you anxious about your parenting skills as well as your child's behavior.

When biting occurs, it begins at about the same age as walking. It happens for a number of reasons. Infants have a strong urge to explore, and since their mouth is the tool they know best, it stands to reason that they put it to use. A child may be observed working his way around a playpen exploring the edge with his mouth: *chomp, chomp, chomp.* It's funny. When he comes across his play-mate's arm—*chomp*—on his way, suddenly it's not funny. Or it may be slightly more deliberate—if I bite the chair arm, nothing happens, but if I bite your arm. . . . Or he may be teething, trying to ease the pressure of swollen gums. Or it may be a child who is struggling unsuccessfully to speak. Unable to say "That toy is mine!" he expresses himself as best he can. Or he may have lost a battle with his older brother at the breakfast table and arrived at the center with a chip on his shoulder. Or, in a few cases, it may be a disgruntled child who welcomes even the negative attention of punishment.

All these reasons for biting exist in infants and toddlers whether they are with their mothers or with a caregiver. However, some reasons for biting may surface only in a specific situation—when a child is with other children his own age. If the toddler described above was in the playpen alone, there would be no biting. If he didn't have to compete with another child for a toy, there might be no biting. If an older brother or sister was present, he or she might interpret for him when adults didn't understand and there might be no biting. That doesn't mean such children have no biting potential, merely that they may have fewer occasions for biting if they are at home alone.

Parents and child care professionals also react to biting and handle biting incidents very differently. Parents of the bitten feel guilt for having placed their child in jeopardy. They may either seek revenge themselves or direct their child to bite back next time. Parents of the biters are cut to the quick. Suddenly their child is transformed into a barbarian, an aggressor. Not only that, they see him as representing family standards of behavior. *They* are guilty of having raised such a child. And other parents may agree.

This is true of almost all parents, by the way, in and out of child care. In a neighborhood, a child who bites is likely to be quickly ostracized by all the families of eligible playmates, possibly along with his parents. He, and they, may not get a chance to work out his problem.

The professional is much more sensitive in dealing with parents. Many center directors will hold a meeting for parents of toddlers at which they warn parents that their child will very probably bite and/or get bitten in the months to come. When an incident does occur, good day-care mothers or center directors will keep in mind the issue of confidentiality and protection of the child and generally will not tell other parents who the biter is, even when pressured. (This won't, of course, prevent a one-year-old victim from pointing out the culprit.)

The professional doesn't blame the biter, either; she matter-of-factly looks for the motive for the biting. An experienced day-care mother or center teacher will watch to see when the biting occurs —it's easy to spot, a child bares his teeth just like a puppy or a kitten—and then will handle the biter according to the problem. A child may be given something cold to soothe swollen gums at critical moments. If the problem is frustration at lack of language, a caregiver may coach the toddler: "This toy is *mine*. Say *mine*." If a biter seems to be intimidating a whole group, she may consider moving him to another, slightly older group. If the problem is one of needing attention, she will see to it that the child gets little or no attention for the incident (aside from being told something along the lines of "We don't bite. Biting hurts people and makes them cry"), but they also try to see that the child gets lots of attention at other times.

Caregivers try to work with all the children too. Some hold up pictures: Can we bite a cookie? Yes. Can we bite an apple? Yes. Can we bite another person? No-o-o-o. (It's exhilarating to watch eight or nine children who are barely verbal, and only hesitantly walking, debating biting. Biting an apple is acceptable, for example, but what about hitting someone over the head with it?)

The caregiver will discuss with the biter's parents what she observes when a child bites, what she does and says in response, and what her next steps will be if present measures are unsuccessful. Whether she comes right out and says it or not, she wants you to do the same in the evenings and on weekends. Maybe some of the triggering events are happening at home.

A parent who listens and tries to cooperate is essential to the caregiver. Look at it from her perspective for a moment: While she accepts biting as a normal, and usually brief, stage of development, she also knows that it will be disruptive while it lasts, hard on all the other children and all the other parents. She's going to get many unhappy phone calls. If a parent won't help to break the cycle, she cannot make all the changes herself, and it is unfair to the other children to expect her to continue with little chance of success.

It's unfortunate that biting is the first tough issue parents and caregiver face together because, in all of child care, it is the hardest on which to cooperate. Since parents are appalled by biting, a caregiver's nonjudgmental assessment of a child's motives will be hard to accept, as will be the idea of doing nothing more than giving positive attention or redirecting a child's attention instead of punishing him. It may help you to involve another professional. If your center director has not had a parent meeting, suggest it. A pediatrician or a specialist in early childhood, sometimes someone from the state licensing agency, may be able to reassure you.

We suggest too that you give yourself some reassurance here. Biting is a short-term problem, and it has nothing to do with how good or bad a parent you are.

TOILET TRAINING:
Easier with Child Care than Without

Like biting, toilet training is a different issue when your child is in child care. But there's a soothing difference. Toilet training in group care is easier for everybody.

A woman who speaks to women's groups throughout the country once said she could establish rapport with an audience instantly: "I just say, 'I bet my son was toilet trained later than any of your kids.'" Instant wave of laughter. And for good reason. You won't get comments about biting unless and until it happens, but when it comes to toilet training, family friends, co-workers, and television call-in shows all tell you what to do. Your parents will tell you you were trained at a year; your husband's parents will counter that he was trained at ten months. (They are both lying.) They give advice whether you ask for it or not; they give it long before a child is physically ready. By a child's second birthday, parents have been burdened with memories, emotions, pressure to succeed, and fear of failing. Your child isn't getting the barrage of helpful hints that you are, but he readily picks up on your complicated feelings. You have all been primed for a difficult time.

Toilet training in child care has none of these pressures. One of the advantages is the group setting. Among other children, a child may become interested in using a toilet almost without realizing it. He can experiment and begin to master this new skill without even realizing that it is one that matters greatly to his parents. The routine that is part of any kind of group care is a big plus in helping a child master toileting skills. A child is always free to use the bathroom at any time, but a teacher or day-care mother also tends to rely on many routines, of which toileting is one, to help organize her day. Everyone washes hands before morning snack, lunch, and afternoon snack, for example; as the weeks and months pass, toileting becomes a part of the routine. Or perhaps everybody visits the bathroom before or after outdoor play. A child gets to watch several times a day; as his own body gets old enough to manage the use of the toilet, he knows where to go, when and how to practice.

The kind of group setting a child is in makes a difference, of course. The children in a day-care home resemble siblings—the age range may include infants up through children in school. This may make imitation less likely. By six, privacy has entered a child's vocabulary, so the two-year-old may never see any behavior to imitate. Then too, if the age disparity is large enough, he may not realize that this is a skill he *can* imitate. Finally, he may fear the older child's teasing.

Believe it or not, the second advantage to toilet training in group care lies in having your child guided by a caregiver instead of by you. You simply aren't there for most of the daytime hours when your child is eating, drinking—and thus needing to use the bathroom. You aren't there to tell if your child is ready to start experimenting. You can no longer be the on-the-scene coach and cheerleader.

Why is this an advantage?

Because your caregiver starts with a perspective different from yours. You begin with the secret fear that your child (and you, the parent) will fail and your child will go to his high school graduation in diapers. Whether she's a sitter or a day-care mother or a teacher or center director, your caregiver begins *knowing* that sooner or later he will succeed.

Caregivers' experience with children has also taught them how success is most apt to come about. They generally mention two things—readiness and attitude. Only part of readiness has to do with a child's age. A second part is language. A child must be able to express her discomfort, even in a single word like *wet,* she must be able to talk about the *potty.* A final part is physical readiness— staying dry for long periods, particularly at night. A child's attitude toward the children who can use the toilet themselves is another indicator—she'll be only casually curious until she's nearly ready to begin imitating them, when she'll begin to watch intently and to focus on the logistics of the skill. (Please note that we are stressing the *child's* curiosity, which is a world away from a parent pointing and saying, "See what Billy can do?")

Finally, a caregiver knows the pattern that leads to success. Despite any stories you have heard of children who look at a toilet, say, "I see," and are trained on the spot, despite books stating that a child can be successfully trained in twenty-four hours, instant success is about as achievable as instant success in driving a car or baking bread. Some children form this new habit sooner than others, but, for all, progress will be ragged. A weather change, a new sibling, moving to a new house, an older sibling who teases, a disappointment sometime during the day—any and all can make toileting an off-again, on-again skill.

Toilet training is a perfect issue on which to learn to work with your caregiver because you will quickly realize that it will take both of you, listening and helping each other, to handle it smoothly. That's true of all the other issues, of course, but because the process for toilet training is clear and easy to follow, it's a good example of how, when you cooperate, you still have a full-time parenting job on your hands.

Since you're not with Billy when he's with other children, how will you know of his newfound curiosity about toileting? Ask your caregiver. She can also tell you if Billy is staying dry for long periods of the day. She may pass on this kind of information to you before you ask. Either way, ask what the next step is. Will she merely observe for a few days (and should you discreetly do the same)? Ask Billy if he wants to try using the toilet? Matter-of-factly assume he wants to without giving him the burden of deciding? Should he begin at the center and then, after a few successes, try at home? Or should you begin at the same time the day-care mother does?

Once again, far more important than the specifics of what you and your caregiver do is the fact that you do the *same* things whenever possible. Has Billy moved from curiosity to experimenting? What times of day does the sitter/day-care mother/child care teacher take him to the bathroom? Is it combined with another routine, like washing hands before lunch or getting up from a nap? When is his dry period during the day? Centers will have an established routine. If your nanny or day-care mother hasn't had one up to now, ask her to take note of when Billy is most successful and to try that time of day on a regular basis.

Once you are on your way to a routine, discuss briefly each evening what has happened that day. A caregiver might say something like, "Billy went at nine, he didn't need to go at eleven, he went before lunch." No more than that—just so that you are up to date.

Use the same language too. It doesn't matter whether you say "potty" or "toilet" or whatever, but it *does* matter that you and your caregiver use the same words. If you don't like slang or baby talk being used for bodily functions, talk about it. A caregiver will try to respect your wishes, but of course there's no guarantee that the other children will—and mastering toilet training is usually followed by a period of silly bathroom talk about both words and process.

How does your caregiver praise for successes? Often it's nothing more than, "Well, that's a big boy." Try to use the same restraint yourself. If the caregiver uses a more obvious reward like a gold star or a sticker on a chart, you may disapprove of that, but you are stuck with it. You can't ask the caregiver to leave out the gold star for only your child because he'll feel discriminated against, and your child may well expect the same reward at home. If so, buy the stars, but you needn't gush over them.

How are accidents handled? Again, we hope without fuss. A caregiver won't let other children make fun of accidents; don't let siblings do so at home.

Be sure to keep the day-care home or center well provided with spare clothing in this period and to keep well up on your laundry at home. When a child can't change quickly and without comment, an accident automatically takes on heightened drama. (If your child has an accident during the day, by the way, you will probably be handed the unrinsed, soiled clothing in a plastic bag at the end of the day. That's not because child care providers don't care for the task of rinsing it out; in many states caregivers are legally forbidden to do so because of the risk of spreading intestinal infections.)

You don't have a child-size toilet as many centers do; a day-care home may use a smaller seat fitted on the toilet, while you use a potty-chair at home. Talk to the teacher/day-care mother about these differences and what you will do at home so that the teacher can refer casually to the stepstool he has at home to reach the toilet or to his own potty-chair. The same goes for you. Take a fresh look at the facilities at the center or day-care home so that you can mention his daytime bathroom. Not discuss, mention—casual comments showing him that you are familiar with all parts of his world and that he is not taking a scary step into outer space.

Most of all, draw on your caregiver's confidence for your own reassurance that sooner or later this skill will be firmly mastered.

SEEING EYE TO EYE WITH YOUR CAREGIVER

We have discussed both biting and toilet training primarily in terms of group child care with professional caregivers, and we've discussed some reasons for doing so—because most children spend time in a group setting by the time these issues arise and because problems occur and can be handled differently in this setting.

There is another reason as well. With these issues, you have experienced the stress of working out problems with a caregiver. To deal with the issues coming up in your child's life, you need a relationship that will survive this stress. And some parents have trouble developing this with a sitter. It may be because she has the experience but is dependent on you, while you, the boss, are inexperienced. Or a sitter may have the same overly personal reactions to biting, the same success/failure approach to toilet training as a parent has. Or the problem may be the insurmountable fact that her ways are a generation or a culture away from your own. (We've heard of more than one housekeeper who routinely used biting as a means of discipline for the biter.)

If your sitter's approach is more easygoing than you would like, adapt to it as much as you comfortably can—the date your son is successfully toilet trained won't appear on his résumé. If she seems intent on quick success, make it clear that that isn't necessary to please you, that you are aware that there will be accidents along the way. If her way is different to a point you consider damaging, though—if she sits a six-month-old on the potty after breakfast till something happens—you must insist that she try your way instead.

This is cooperation of a kind, but it is a long step away from the reassurance a professional caregiver can give. In the next chapter, we'll discuss your child's main occupation in the months and years to come: learning how to function in a group—working and playing with others, sticking up for himself, making friends. As you embark on this period, it may be time to take a fresh look at your child's needs and your caregiver's ability to meet them—and to help you meet them.

CHAPTER TEN

BECOMING PART OF A GROUP:

The Third and Fourth Year

. . . .

Some morning near her second birthday, that gentle child of yours will shake her curls, fold her arms and say, "No!" and repeat it, at a rising decibel level, till she has to be marched inside, or outside, or sat down—plump!—to have her suddenly despised boots pulled on. The clash between her needs and the rules of the universe in which she lives has begun.

Like sitting and standing and walking, she will make so many strikes at asserting herself that you'll have plenty of chances to appreciate firsthand why two-year-olds are so often labeled terrible. Human juggernauts, they are so helpless before their own needs and energy that they cannot easily control themselves. Adults, children, or anything that gets in the way is treated as an obstacle. It's because a two-year-old's reach so often exceeds her grasp; and that, in turn, is because two-year-olds are growing unevenly in a dozen different directions. Growth has become a very chaotic business.

The uneven growth that makes frustration so inevitable for a child is baffling to parents too. Instead of the tidy progression of growth steps that you have become used to (sit, then stand, then walk), suddenly many things begin to develop simultaneously. From this point on, a child's growth will be more of a flow, with no iron-clad rules for the order or pace at which things are mastered.

That means we have to discuss it differently too. We're going to describe significant *areas* of achievement, how most children handle them at the beginning of this period and again at the end, when they are rounding out their fourth year and ready for kindergarten. We'll talk about how parent and caregiver can work together to make this a productive time—and what happens when they work at cross purposes.

There's a second, possibly even a more important, change in the way a child grows now. While babies and toddlers concentrate on personal skills like sitting and walking, from the late two's on, almost everything a child does is in some way connected to a group. By the age of three, most centers group children according to the cut-off birth dates for school in their community. This is possible in part because around three, most children have begun to do the same things at the same ages, but it's also both a signal and a recognition of the growing importance of a peer group.

Parents too recognize that a child needs other children; by this age, most children are in some form of group care for some part of their day. That doesn't mean that you are free of misgivings about child care, but your concerns are different. Instead of debating in-home versus group care, you worry about what happens when the group a child is struggling to become part of is in a child care setting rather than under your eagle eye. Will a caregiver have the skill to make these years the positive, creative time they can be, or will she settle for preventing mayhem? What does a child miss when she spends all day every day in a group? Will she turn into just a face in the crowd? Will the group somehow take over for the family? Your relationship with your caregiver—and hers with you—has to expand to deal with such concerns.

WHEN GROWTH COMES IN GIANT STEPS

This whole period is marked by a triumphant surge of *language*. One aspect of the struggle of a two-year-old is that "No" has to stand for too many needs and feelings. As a child learns to communicate how she feels and thinks and what she wants to do more clearly, many other kinds of growth become possible and "No" fades away.

Language skills will expand faster in a group setting. A child has more people to talk to and more activities to talk to them about. She's exposed to more vocabulary. Each family has its own; in a group setting she's exposed to a dozen families' worth of words daily. And the faster her language skills increase, the faster she can do a host of other things. The child whose vocabulary seemed confined to "No" will have language enough for daydreams and arguments within two short years; she'll have friends, letters, numbers, and games at her command.

One of the things language makes possible over this period is *fantasy*. A three-year-old can't really articulate one, but as she falls in love with words, she goes on and on about what happens at home, at the center—and if it's a good story, she just keeps on going. Real and imaginary mingle for a while. One four-year-old, describing to another the wolf who lived in his attic, said conscientiously, "It's an imaginary wolf." He paused, then added, "But the *gorilla* is real." Deliberate lies become part of this too. Experts feel that the ability to tell a lie and know one is doing so is an important and positive stage in a child's independence. By the end of the fourth year, they'll know fantasy from truth from fibs and use all appropriately. They'll even share fantasies, happily acting out together adventures with dinosaurs and soldiers.

Sharing is one of the big tasks of this period. When you see two two-year-olds playing together peacefully, don't be deceived. They are playing *beside* one another and you've caught a moment when their needs don't happen to collide. As she approaches three, the group in which a child can function may increase from two to three or four, but each is still playing independently of the others. If three three-year-olds are in the kitchen area of a playroom, for example, one may be banging saucepans, a second exploring the refrigerator, a third washing dishes. Since each activity is bound to fascinate the others, very soon the pan-banger pushes the dishwasher out of the way and says, *"I want!"* At this point the teacher intervenes to avert war.

That is the beginning of sharing. It is undoubtedly a learned activity. Look at all that goes into it: You don't push or shove or hit; you don't take away a toy. You must respect another child's space—if she is at the stove, you don't push her away to take possession of it; if she is sitting on a chair, you don't push her off.

All these are rules, and learning rules is a major activity at this age. It begins with sharing but spreads far beyond. That is, children who have learned the rules against pushing and shoving can use that knowledge to go out to the playground peacefully; once there, their growing awareness of rules makes possible more complicated games—relays, cowboys and Indians, even jump rope. When they work on projects, their ability to follow the rules for being careful as well as their growing motor skills make possible work with scissors and glue. More grown-up behavior makes possible more grown-up games and tasks.

Another important component of sharing is what we define as *trust*. When a child trusts the world in which she lives, she finds it easier to learn many things. Trust lies behind self-control: three-year-olds have a lot of trouble sitting still; four-year-olds, though they're much more physically active, can handle it because they trust that their turn will come. Trust makes it easier to master sequence, or a sense of what comes next: I don't have to talk *right now;* I can do it *later.* Most of all, it's comfort in one's environment: If I wait, I know "they'll" see that I get a turn too. Three-year-olds need help to take turns; four-year-olds have forgotten it was ever any other way.

HELPING YOUR CHILD LEARN SELF-MASTERY

For both parents and caregivers, the job throughout this period is to help a child who is little more than an infant develop the poise and the polished skills of the four-year-old. But they approach it differently. The parents are at the center of the child's world and are dealing with only one child. A teacher, in contrast, is always working with a group of children. Children generally will try to conform to the behavior of the group. The child who eats what everybody else does at lunchtime may have a temper tantrum over whatever you serve him that night. It's safer and more private to test you.

Let's use "No" again to illustrate the differences between parents' approach and caregivers'. A parent, if he or she chooses to do so, can use physical means to make a child obey. A licensed center or day-care mother cannot: Physical or corporal punishment of any kind is forbidden by most state regulations. Of *any* kind. If another child hits or bites yours, hitting or biting back won't be allowed. There will be no punishment related to food or naps, no dunce caps, no demeaning of the child.

Caregivers universally find that parents have trouble throughout this stage. The process, to parents, can be summed up by the word *discipline.* This is the issue parents say they consider the most important, the one they talk about most—and, interestingly, the quality about group child care that parents most often single out for praise.

We think the difficulty of this stage may lie in large part in the way parents define it. In infancy and toddlerhood, most of a child's achievements are things to applaud and perhaps coach—there isn't much of a down side. In this stage, though, the issues of a child's life affect the parents too. Most see them as they do toilet training, in terms of success and failure. A child *must* learn the rules of the world. "They think their child is a square peg," said one center director, "and they see their job as making that peg fit into a round hole."

People in the child care field looking at the same period of growth see something very different, a difference expressed in the words they use. They rarely use the term *discipline,* saying instead *behavior management* or *positive redirection.* They see discipline as *self*-discipline, self-mastery. Self-mastery isn't a head-to-head conflict. It's the child's struggle to build self-esteem. That, in turn, makes it possible for a child to begin the all-important task of finding her place in a group.

Thus, when a child first says "No" and parents first see the need for discipline, caregivers see instead the child's frustration. Children are not adults; they don't see a problem in terms of who's right or wrong; nor are they seeking a moral resolution. Caregivers handle it by diverting or redirecting them. If a toddler has somehow made herself miserable in the block corner, her teacher will take her over to the kitchen and together they'll check out the refrigerator. If two children are contesting ownership of a truck, she'll tempt one of them with a doll in a cradle. If a child is trying to throw blocks, a teacher will substitute bean bags and a target. Redirection is particularly effective with two-year-olds, who are almost helpless in the face of their own energy. (All of this, by the way, can be done without explanation or criticism.)

Then there's the "No" that means "I want to do it myself and I can't yet!" A child who seems to be willfully playing Animal House at the snack table is probably just unskillful. In this case, the assumption will be that she needs help. A caregiver might tell her to eat more slowly or show her how to hold her fork or tuck in her napkin or help her put on an apron.

Sometimes a child's scream of outrage is, to her, justified. To a child still learning the uses of language, hearing the words "Would you like to . . . ?" when she really has no choice about going to Grandma's or the supermarket is maddening. A caregiver will rarely make that mistake. When a child honestly doesn't have a choice, she won't be offered one; she will be told that it's time to wash her hands for snack or put on her jacket to go outside without being asked if she'd like to go.

For conflicts between children, when redirection and diversion aren't sufficient, there are negotiations. In some centers, teachers have established "talk-it-over" chairs. To settle disagreements, they pull out chairs and sit the disputing children down knee to knee and walk through the conversation with them. Three-year-olds can struggle through this negotiation with lots of teacher support; four-year-olds will actually go get the chairs themselves.

When a child behaves in a way that pulls the whole group apart, a caregiver is apt to place her away from the others for a few minutes. (It's usually called time out.) A toddler, who doesn't really understand what the concept is about and can't sit still anyway, might be placed briefly just outside the group; three- and four-year-olds would be asked to sit apart from the group (but still under the teacher's eye) for roughly a minute per year of age.

Caregivers say they use this positive, patient, low-key approach because it works, and that's true. Can parents—who, after all, have both a more intense relationship with their child and different goals for her—use it as well?

Actually, this low-key approach can benefit parents a great deal —but for very different reasons than it does a caregiver.

The first reason is purely practical. Your caregiver is your resident expert. If you choose to take the same approach, you have access to an expert every day for help, advice, even coaching. You can watch what she does and what the results are any time you choose; you can ask how she handles behaviors and situations that puzzle you. If you fear your four-year-old son is overly aggressive, and his teacher says, "Oh, yes, the young stallion phase!" it becomes much easier for you to take his headlong activity in stride. She may recommend ways to cope that fit in with this approach but can't be followed at a center. On a day when nothing pleases a child, for example, she might suggest a long bath before bedtime. Caregivers welcome such questions and conversations. It indicates respect for their experience.

The second reason a low-key approach is a good choice for parents is that the alternatives can be disastrous.

When parents make too big a fuss, whether by overpraising or overshaming or overblaming, the child quickly focuses on the intensity of the emotion and learns that saying no or refusing to eat or pushing another child off a chair is a bad thing to do. The consequences of that knowledge depend on the child. A fearful child will have more trouble with mastery; an aggressive child may use her table manners or her disobedience as a way of getting back at her parents much as a toddler will hold her breath. The parents react with more shame or blame, the child reacts to the parents' reaction by being even more fearful or more headstrong; parents and child can quickly lock into a tight, unhappy circle of repetitive behavior.

That can happen if you've made a poor child care choice too, of course—teachers can label a child a bully or a clown and by the label help to create one. But you can break that cycle quickly and absolutely by moving your child someplace else. Parents and children, on the other hand, can keep on repeating destructive behaviors for a lifetime.

That has always been true for parents and children, but child care has changed the equation. Before child care, children locked into patterns of blame or shame or bribery or punishment accepted it as normal—it was the only pattern they knew. Now they are exposed to different methods during the day.

What does that mean? When you and your caregiver take the same approach, no bells and whistles go off to reassure you that you've done the right thing. But when you don't work together, you force your child to accept a crazy picture of the world. If pushing somebody is treated firmly but matter-of-factly from eight to five each day but on evenings and weekends invites a dramatic lecture or offers of clothes for her Cabbage Patch doll if she'll stop, your child must master two sets of rules at the same time. Consistency between caregiver and home is very important.

If a child's eyes cross from the strain and she decides to give up trying to learn anything at all, we wouldn't blame her. If she manages to learn to function in a group under these conditions, she will also have learned that she must use one set of rules with you and another set with others. The penalties for her, and for you, will be very great.

WHAT CONCERNS PARENTS MOST ABOUT GROUP CARE

Common tasks, common discipline—do you get an image of a group of children all moving in lockstep? That's the picture that makes parents mistrustful of large child care centers and dubious about children spending all their days in group care. It's an inside-out way of expressing the goals parents have for their children in these years. That is, by saying, I don't want my child to be a member of a pack, a parent is also saying, I want my child to be creative, or to have one-on-one friendships, or to be a leader.

These are legitimate fears. Children at this age need to practice leadership and friendship; they need private time to digest what they are learning and think about who they are. You, in turn, must be satisfied that your caregiver is sensitive to these needs and that they can be met by the child care you have chosen.

Here's a rundown of the most common worries, plus responses you have a right to expect from your caregiver.

Parents worry that children in group child care all day will have *no time to themselves.* Although functioning within a group is by far the most powerful theme of these years, children do stretch abilities within themselves as well as with others. Three-year-olds, for example, have trouble solving problems; if the solution isn't immediately apparent, they'll whine or lose their tempers. Four-year-olds have learned to persist until they succeed. As with sharing, they have learned to trust—in this case, in themselves. It takes time and space to develop that trust—time to read or even to talk to themselves, perhaps to read or talk to a toy; to curl up and dream. "Cogitating," one center director calls it. In a well-run group setting, there should be places and spaces for a child to be alone— library areas with big pillows and books, sometimes fabric hangings that mark off an area for quiet play.

Parents today also worry about *boys and girls being treated in stereotypical ways.* In some ways, that's easier to avoid in group care. Materials are nonsexist—books describe tasks and adventures even-handedly, posters show both men and women as firefighters, police officers, and doctors.

But there's more to stereotypes than that. Whatever kind of caregiver you have, she'll reflect the behavior customary in the part of the country in which you live. For better, for worse. A babysitter a generation older than you will have the views of her generation rather than yours. A babysitter fifteen years younger may have an athletic, street-wise approach that with the best of intentions you find unwomanly. Sometimes religious views color the way girls and boys are treated.

As important as the way caregivers treat children is the way they treat and are treated by adults. If a center director describes and treats her teachers with respect, she's setting up a model for respect for women. If you describe and treat your caregiver with respect, so are you.

Many parents fear that children who are always in a big group, guided by adults all day long, won't ever have a chance to *organize and invent their own play* as they might in their own backyard.

If you need reassurance on this one, take the time to observe a class of three- or four-year-olds. They rarely do anything as a group; instead, they continually break off into what one director calls "subcolonies" of two or three or four children. And although a preschool should have a program, it should be fluid enough so that children have a choice of activities that they can follow at different attention spans and vary as they choose. Where one subgroup may devote lengthy, serious time to putting kernels of corn on placards with squares for numbers, a second group may use the same cards and corn to set up an imaginary battlefield or castle. Most of the time, too, children should have the independence to choose which activity they want to do and when, and as in your own backyard, one of their favorite activities will be taking turns laying down the law to one another.

Just as in neighborhood play, subcolonies nearly always sort themselves out into the same few children. This should be comforting to parents who fear that a group setting interferes with one of the richest pleasures of this age: *making friends*. Three-year-olds try to be friends with one another. They can be very tender. If a child falls or doesn't feel well, it's almost as though the others have a sixth sense alerting them to his discomfort as they ask how he feels or give him a comforting pat.

But it's not until a child learns to function within a group— taking turns, sharing games, telling other children stories—that she becomes aware enough of the others to be drawn to those who are interested in the same things and work at the same speed. Four-year-olds are buddies. Ask your child tonight whom she plays with most; ask her again in a week and in three months. Chances are her favorites will be the same.

When friendships do change, though, the shift is a lot easier in group care than it is in your backyard. For one thing, because there are more children to choose from, a fight doesn't leave a child bereft of playmates. She doesn't have to give in to keep a friend. And since both children are still in the same room day in and day out, they will have endless chances to begin playing together again without having to negotiate or establish blame or apologize.

Whatever your choice of group care, then, you can be reassured that your child will be able to make friends. That's the positive side. Parents worry even more about the dark side of friendship in child care—the possibility that their child may make *a friend they dislike* and that they will be powerless to bring the friendship to an end.

There's no question that if you are at home, you have absolute control over your child's choice of friends before she is in school. You dial the phone, you drive the car—if you don't approve of a child, you can easily find her too inconvenient to play with. Exercising similar control from your workplace through a caregiver is unquestionably more difficult. The prickliest situation is when you don't approve of a child taken care of by a friend of your nanny or sitter. You can forbid them to play together, but you can't guarantee that you will be obeyed—or in what spirit you will be obeyed. "I wish you could play with Linda too, but your Mommy said no," undercuts what you are trying to do in a damaging way. It's just as difficult to curtail a friendship if your child is one of a small group taken care of by a sitter or day-care mother. You are, in effect, asking her to choose between two clients.

In group care, you have a better chance that things will work out in your favor. Although children play in groups of two or three, they choose from a group of around a dozen. Observers say that parents can rest assured that children reflect their parents' standards even when the parents aren't there. You'll frequently hear comments like "My mother says we don't eat with our fingers" or "My daddy says we don't play with guns."

A center director will also try to honor a parent's wishes to the degree that it's possible. That is, if she can redirect a child, she will. She is probably not, however, going to ask another child to withdraw from the center, nor is she going to let the whole class be disrupted by having a teacher separate two children who clamor to be together.

A director may also encourage you to spend some time watching the play with a friend you don't care for. The friendship may be satisfying something your child needs. Frequently a cautious child tags after a child who hurtles through the day headlong, for example. Since the cautious child may have cautious parents, they're probably not pleased. But the child may in fact be using caution—using the risk taker "almost like a guinea pig," said one mother after she had watched a while. "She lets her try something and then if it works out, my daughter tries it too." That doesn't mean that you need to encourage a relationship that disturbs you, but try to pin down its appeal to your child. If you can find other ways to meet that need, the friendship may wither without further action.

Finally, remember that children must learn to live with many different kinds of people, and they become stronger as they do so.

A friend you don't happen to care for is light-years away from a still more serious concern—a *bully/victim* relationship. The fear of raising either bully or victim is probably the greatest fear parents have for a child in a group setting. A child who harasses others and so is never chosen for a friend, or a child who is regularly picked on by others—these images haunt all our dreams at one time or another. And, of course, they happen, but not often. A center with a hundred children probably has a bully—but probably not more than one.

In the case of bullies and victims, the problem is not just one of tastes or family standards or personalities. These are children with some learning to do. Both need to learn the rules of respecting a child's space, whether one's own or another child's. The bully needs to improve her sense of time and trust—that she can wait and that she will eventually get a turn. She needs to learn that sweet, passive children have as many rights as boisterous ones. The victim needs to learn that she has choices—that she can choose to use a toy—and probably also to recognize when she is trespassing on somebody else's rights. Victims are often inexperienced children who don't see the implications of taking another child's ball. Both need to rely more on the sharing of feelings—to describe their desire to play with a doll and to defend a right to keep using it. A teacher may actually walk through that conversation, not once but many times.

With a sitter or housekeeper, the best way to control access to unwanted friends is to add part-time group care of some kind to your child's schedule, whether nursery school or a child care center. Take the time to observe the kids, focus on the ones you like, and arrange for play in the afternoons away from school. In other words, fill your child's schedule with children you like rather than forbidding a playmate. (It's the idea of redirection rather than confrontation again, this time applied to your sitter.)

THE GROWING IMPORTANCE OF NEIGHBORHOOD

One last point about children's friendships: A child needs friends in her own neighborhood now. That means that if your child has been in on-site child care in your workplace, you may think seriously now about looking for care closer to where you live. Some workplaces are near home, but most are not, and on-site centers draw children from all directions and distances. That didn't matter when she was a baby, but now your child needs friends with whom she will play on Saturday and Sunday afternoons, have identical sweatshirts, ride bicycles around the block and eventually —most importantly—go to kindergarten.

It's just as important for you to meet the parents of these friends and to learn the unwritten ins and outs of your local school system, from the favorite teachers to the best Brownie troop. In California, a recent law makes it possible for parents to register their children for schools in the district in which they work, but of course we won't know for years how well that will work. For now, you'd better plan to plug into the existing neighborhood network.

If your child is in family day care or with a group babysitter, it's time to reexamine that choice as well. Although it's good for children to be with a range of ages, in the third and fourth year it is much more important to spend time with one's own age group. A child needs to see other children in similar situations, facing similar problems. They need inspiration, to be able to copy behaviors and solutions appropriate to their age; they need the comfort of knowing that others too have to struggle—and they need to make friends.

C H A P T E R E L E V E N

SPECIAL EVENTS:

Celebrations and Character Builders
. . . .

So far, we have been talking about growth stages that all children share, but other events in a child's life may be unique to him and his family. They are out of his control and may be out of the control of his parents as well.

Some are physical, like learning to live with glasses or braces or surgery or allergies. Others are events that a child is powerless to influence and uncertain how to live with, like moving or divorce or a parent's remarriage (possibly including stepbrothers and stepsisters), or the death of a grandparent, or the birth of a new baby. Being a sibling or an only child presents challenges when a child is in child care. Finally, there's the role of celebrations and holidays —they mark the ways in which a child begins to see himself as a citizen, of his family and his culture.

You can't shield your child from such events, nor would you want to. They are what make a child a Muscari or Morrone or

Smith or Jones. What's more, said one child psychiatrist, "the struggle to make sense of them builds character."

That doesn't mean, though, that a child can take them in stride. We doubt that you can either. We are going to describe for you what will help a child, his parents, and his caregiver through these special events. If a sitter or center director has strong ideas and they're different from ours, that doesn't make either of us right or either of us wrong. Listen carefully and work with what you can. A single approach, even one that hadn't occurred to you, will be better for your child than double messages.

We are confident you already have a good working relationship with your sitter or day-care mother or center director because these are not ideal issues through which to develop one. If not, you'll just have to brace yourself and plunge in because your child needs guidance from both of you to cope with any of these problems.

PHYSICAL PROBLEMS

A child may have to cope with a physical problem like very poor vision, a crossed eye because of a weak eye muscle, poor speech because of an orthodontic problem, hearing loss from constant ear infections, or tonsils that become infected often.

One of the advantages of group care, by the way, is the exhaustive health records that licensed centers are required to keep. A child is measured against norms more frequently than he would be by a sitter or housekeeper—or even a pediatrician once a child is more than a year old. Health problems like hearing loss or too-slow growth are frequently picked up earlier, when correction may be easier and may avert damaging side-effects. The most common example of this is the hearing loss caused by constant ear infections. It is sometimes corrected by a simple surgical procedure —small tubes are inserted through the eardrum to drain the jammed Eustachian tubes—but if it isn't detected and corrected before the surge in language that begins late in the second year, all the growth dependent on speech, from fantasy to making friends, will be slowed. If the problem isn't caught till kindergarten, some children will struggle in vain to make up the lost ground. Some directors have seen more dramatic cases, like early detection of muscular dystrophy or cystic fibrosis.

Physical problems like those above are corrected in one of two ways—apparatus, such as glasses or dental headgear, and minor surgery, such as inserting tubes in the ears. Though the problems they correct are about equally serious, the treatments present quite different obstacles to a child.

Surgery represents the unknown. Even when he's told that it will be minor, even when he knows (or *hopes* he knows) that he'll be more comfortable afterward, it is probably the most frightening thing that has happened in his life so far. Minor surgery may mean being separated from you for the first time. You can't promise that there won't be pain.

How can your caregiver help you? If you talk over the problem beforehand, she in turn can deal with the problem in class. It can be enormously helpful to discuss it during Circle Time, particularly if she knows of a similar medical event in somebody else's family, but that is your decision—she will never do it without your permission. If the center regularly takes a hospital tour as a field trip, she may be familiar with the routines and the layout—perhaps even personnel—and can refer to them in reassuring ways. If she sees your child spending lots of unaccustomed time off by himself and knows the reason, she has some idea of how to begin and guide a conversation. Because she isn't as important to him as you are, he may not feel as compelled to put up a brave front to her. Because you are (unavoidably) the one proposing the corrective surgery, he may have more trouble discussing fears with you than with someone who isn't involved. Just as mother and father generally take on unique roles, so the caregiver, with her all-day everyday practice in talking about feelings, may have a special role to play too. If so, try to be grateful, not jealous—a child in need needs all the help he can get.

So do you. Ask the director of the child care center to keep you informed of any conversations. He may have fears that haven't occurred to you (do they turn the lights off in a hospital at night, do they allow soda or ice cream, can my mommy stay with me). If any other children in the center have had similar problems, does she have happy-ending stories you can share with your child? Books to recommend? (Two we like: *Madeleine* and *Curious George Goes to the Hospital.)*

Surgery, however minor the parents know it to be, means bracing oneself for the unknown. If your child faces instead corrective apparatus like glasses or orthodontic headgear or a bite block that muffles his speech temporarily, he copes with another, equally painful obstacle: fear of being different. Four eyes, R2D2, mocking imitations of his lisp: Your imagination paints them all too vividly.

You may be relieved to learn that parents usually have more trouble with this than their preschoolers do. There are two reasons for it. What most parents don't realize is that some medical procedures that they think will cause a child to be treated like a freak have become fairly common. Orthodontia, for example, has changed enormously since today's parents were children. In 1971, 75 percent of orthodontic correction was done during the teens by pulling four permanent teeth and shifting the rest of the teeth to fit. By 1981, 80 percent was *not* done that way. Now treatment is done early, while the bones are growing. Palate wideners, stretching the upper jaw to make room for all expected teeth, are common, and correction may begin in the fourth year. Thus, if a child is wearing headgear that looks like something out of a Star Wars movie, there's a chance that he may not be alone—there may be a fellow-sufferer in another class or somebody will have a brother or sister similarly strapped up.

Then too, children at this age have a great deal of compassion for one another. We have seen children coping with the hair loss of chemotherapy or with injuries leading to gross facial disfigurement who are accepted within a day or two. Not quite matter-of-factly —three- and four-year-olds are routinely protective of children who are limited in some way. A director describes seeing one boy go up to another, catch him by the shoulders and say something nose to nose. Sensing an argument, she asked if there was a problem. Startled, the boy looked up, then shook his head: "You have to get close and let Benjie watch what you say," he explained— and then the director remembered that Benjie had severe hearing loss. The teasing that parents have in mind really begins with older children, sometime in second and third grade.

SPECIAL EVENTS

Moving, divorce, remarriage, an illness of somebody close, and the birth of a new baby are dramatic changes. Even when parents see an event as good, it's still something that a child must come to terms with. That sometimes takes parents aback, and they react with impatience rather than understanding.

While moving is difficult for children, you will probably get more good advice for this event than for any other. For one thing, it's so common. Families move every five to seven years. When children are of infant to preschool age, their families are bound to shift, either from a small apartment to a larger one, or from an apartment to a house; add to that the shifts related to job moves of one or both parents.

This means everybody—including your child—has lots of experience with moving. He has welcomed new children and waved good-bye to friends. If he brings up the move in Circle Time (or if you give the teacher permission to do so), there are bound to be other children who have just moved or are, like you, about to do so. As with minor surgery, sharing the unknown makes it less frightening.

The teacher's experience is even more valuable. She has listened to more fears than you could even imagine. A common one: never seeing his toys again. Assure him that a box of his favorites will travel with him rather than in the van (which as far as he knows is driving off into outer space).

There are also ways to help ease the change. First, there's celebrating all he has loved about where he is now. Help him make a list of the things he most wants to remember. The teacher may ask him to bring in pictures of favorite times. If you're moving out of the area, take pictures of favorite places and of the children who will be left behind (with the center director's permission).

Then there's making friends with the new. If you are moving to a house you've already chosen, take a picture of it into the center for all the children to look at. Draw a map of the area, with Magic Marker trails to parks, malls, library. Do you have a picture or even a rough drawing of his new room? Where will his toys go? Where will his bed go? Where will the dog sleep? Where will the tortilla chips be stored in the kitchen?

If you're moving to a new area and you won't choose your house till you're there, then use, instead, a map of the area, emphasizing things the family can do together—a drive along a river, the possibility of a yard big enough for a dog, a zoo, a hands-on museum.

A center may be able to help *you* too. At Kinder-Care, the director of your present center will write to the area where you're moving, telling the regional director to expect you. Your child can be placed in a center in the new area while you're house hunting (even though that may not be the center you will finally decide to use). Any company with several centers that can lend you similar support will certainly do so. It's not always possible, of course—in which case, turn to Chapter 8 (page 112) for suggestions of how to bridge the gap in child care while you find a house, settle into a new routine, and decide what kind of care you need. If you're planning a move within your present area, ask center directors for their opinion of various school districts before you begin house hunting. Since they do prekindergarten testing and transport school-age children to and from schools, they get to know them.

The fact that your child has already had some form of child care will help to smooth the way the next time. He knows the ropes now. That doesn't mean he won't be apprehensive and fearful— expect longer naps for a while—but he knows what to expect.

An indispensable book here: *Good-bye, House* by Ann Banks and Nancy Evans (Harmony Books).

FAMILY TRAGEDIES

Other events, though perhaps no more disruptive to a child's life, can be harder to handle both because there are fewer guidelines and because parents don't share them. Many parents don't tell their caregiver about the serious illness or death of a close relative, for example. Some children act out openly with bouts of tears, lots of talk, renewed demands for a beloved blanket they had put away; a caregiver who knows just what's wrong recognizes the signals for help. But other children turn inward or show signs of anger or a spike of allergic reactions instead of grief. Unless the parents explain the problem, a caregiver has few clues as to what's wrong or what to do beyond her own intuition and experience.

The word really must come from you. Children of this age will say anything in Circle Time. A new baby sister? Maybe it's true, and maybe your husband really is a firefighter, and maybe you do have a gorilla in the attic. A caregiver will take it with a grain of salt until *you* tell her.

Any family tragedy, from divorce to death, is a personal matter; no responsible caregiver is going to tell you what you should and should not do. She will probably bend over backward to try to help in whatever way you feel is best.

A caregiver may also point out some easily avoided pitfalls. Since it's difficult to explain death to children this age, parents commonly say, "It's like going to sleep." But this is a literal age. One boy whose grandfather had died suddenly became a pest at rest time, going from child to child and lifting up their eyelids to see if they were still "there." Another child might fear going to sleep himself. Instead of saying something that sounds comforting to *you,* it's best to find out what the child's questions are really about. Is he afraid his grandfather was in pain? that a parent will disappear with the same lack of warning? that he will be next? Is he having trouble putting into words his own sense of loss? Many caregivers excel in helping children talk about feelings. Can she advise you, even down to specific phrasing? (A question beginning with "Why" is threatening, for example.)

A caregiver can offer some practical help. In the case of separation or divorce, for example, a caregiver can tell you that boys almost always become much more aggressive. (This is so predictable that one expert even suggests that the family move after the worst is over, to give a boy a fresh start where other children won't remember his behavior.) She also knows which of the other children in the class lives with only one parent. Even though they may not be on your child's current list of friends, perhaps his circle could widen to include children of other single-parent families. He may be able to ask them questions he can't ask an adult—or they may just give him a feeling of protective coloration. Perhaps more important, the parents can be a resource for you in the confusing new life you have begun. You may need car pool help you haven't needed before, back-ups for evening pick-up. A caregiver can tell you where potential snags lie and how others have coped with them—but only if she knows what's going on.

There is also help a caregiver should *not* give. Child care—particularly if outside the home—can be for a child an oasis of sameness in a world made turbulent by his parents' separation and divorce. But it's not always easy for parents to keep hands off. As they do elsewhere in their lives during this difficult period, parents frequently try to draw their caregiver into taking sides. Even if the caregiver can be persuaded to do so, though, it just diminishes the support she can offer your child. Caregivers can't advise you about legal steps; they are not marriage counselors; they can't report to one spouse on what the other spouse is doing or with whom or on their fitness as a parent. Will the noncustodial spouse still be allowed to pick up your child? If not, that's your decision, not the caregiver's, and you must get a notarized court order to back you up.

NEW PARENTS, NEW SIBLINGS

Events like remarriage (possibly with a mix of children) or a new baby that seem positive to the parents may seem less so to the child. Some of the incidents that happen to you will make funny stories years from now too—trading the baby for a puppy and so on. Naturally you have planned to be patient. But it's hard to accept jealousy that goes on day in and day out, particularly when you too are adjusting to a new relationship or a new child. Patience is in short supply.

Caregivers should be informed of a new marriage, if only to update the list of people allowed to pick up your child. This will also help your caregiver to help your child to adjust. A caregiver may suggest that Brian bring in his new daddy and introduce him to the other kids. She'll point out other children who have new daddies. As with the handling of a parent moving out, sharing the event with other children, under the caregiver's guidance, accomplishes several things. It gives your child a support group; it shows him that he is still acceptable; and it helps him find acceptable ways of expressing and living with his feelings without hammering them out on you.

BROTHERS AND SISTERS IN CHILD CARE

A sibling relationship starts with the adjustment to a new baby, but it doesn't end there. We think this is an overlooked and terribly important issue. We must find ways of helping our children connect to one another as brother and sister even though they spend their days in child care.

Some families see this as a much more difficult task than others. One mother of a two- and a five-year-old, both in group child care since birth in a small neighborhood center, suggests that the parents' confidence is the most important element. If there is a lot of family time—an active church role, vacations spent together, weekend trips—and there is clearly a strong value attached to the family, then child care doesn't present a problem; it's just one part of their lives. On the other hand, if a family is stretched to the limit in all directions and time together is spent trying desperately to catch up, then all the family relationships will seem diluted.

Nevertheless, let's consider how you can underline the time your children spend together. Some parents arrange for it by having a housekeeper or nanny, with group care beginning as a part-time activity when the older child turns three or four. This frequently works very well. But it is a complicated mix of relationships, as we have pointed out elsewhere. It's also expensive, and it isn't readily available in many parts of the country.

Other families have been able to handle the relationships within group care. When children are in different settings, one mother recommends that the whole family deliver the younger in the morning, taking a few minutes for him to show what he's working on. In the afternoon, reverse the process, picking up the younger first and taking him with you into the older child's center so that *he* can show off a bit.

If both children are in the same center, you will want a director who shares your goals, so be upfront about them from the very beginning. Within the center's routine, there are many ways to help siblings to connect. Although the infant room is usually separate from the other open space of a center for health reasons, older children are encouraged to visit "their" babies, and there are big windows through which they can watch when the babies are awake and even point out activities to other children. Once the younger child is a toddler, a center can help siblings to cross paths. One class can pass through another's to get to the playground. The two classes may be scheduled to go to the playground at the same time so that brother and sister can keep track of each other. If either older or younger is going through a rocky time for some reason, the other child may sometimes be given time in his class. They may share rest times for a while. And be assured, say directors, children do know when their siblings are unhappy; when the calm sibling is allowed to comfort the needy one, both are soothed.

Part of what is happening here is an affirmation of family. But there is also the role of being an older child or a younger child. Both are important. It matters for the older child to have a sense of bigness, of being compassionate. It matters that the younger have a sense of being looked after, of his own personal role model.

This is true for children other than siblings, of course, which is one of the advantages of having a sitter who cares for several children or (on a more formal basis) a day-care mother. A good child care center will try to get the best of both worlds by having family groupings within the center at the beginning and the end of the day, or having older children occasionally help with younger.

ONLIES AND FIRSTBORNS

The children for whom it's probably most important to practice older/younger relationships are only children. Then again, they are also the children for whom it is of paramount importance to spend time with children their own age. As yet, there aren't studies comparing how only children develop in and out of group child care, but we do know that parents of only children are among the greatest boosters of group child care.

They mention the importance of other children for the only child to imitate. The times at which a child rolls over, sits, pulls himself up to stand, talks, and walks are inborn. But how he does it and how often, when he tries a slide or swing may come from watching another child and realizing that it can be done. Language is richer with children as well as adults contributing words and style and subjects of discussion. Only children will do each of these things earlier in group child care than they will with a sitter.

This is different from children being pushed by their parents to master things as early as possible. An only child pushes himself in group care in part because ideas occur to him that might not at home; in part because he sees other children try things and survive and so can assess their risk realistically; probably most of all, say parents, because he's not bored. Only children tend to dash impatiently into child care on Monday morning. Parents say they find the weekends drag; they want to see some of their playmates over the weekend. Unlike only children with in-home care, they spend their days in a child's, rather than an adult's world. They relish it.

The long-term implications of this will affect all of us, as will changes in another group: oldest children. The more recent studies of only children link their character traits to those of firstborn children, and it is from these groups that we draw a disproportionate number of our leaders, from presidents of corporations to generals. What will happen to both these groups when their childhood is spent in a group, with an emphasis on cooperation and companionship? We do know that children get a chance to practice leadership in center-based child care.

CELEBRATIONS

Finally, there are special occasions. Some are personal, like birthdays. Others have largely lost their original meaning and seem to serve principally to divide the calendar—Valentine's Day, St. Patrick's Day, Halloween. Still others are national—Thanksgiving, Presidents' Day, the Fourth of July. Finally, there are religious holidays, like Christmas, Easter, Chanukah, Yom Kippur.

Almost all kinds of child care celebrate birthdays. If your religion forbids it, as Jehovah's Witnesses do, for example, you may be best off with a sitter or with child care within your church. It's extremely hard for a child to watch those around him mark off their special days when he is never to have one of his own. There will probably be a special hat, and you will be allowed to provide a treat for snack—though in many states, health codes require that it be store-bought rather than homemade. Check well in advance to see how a center or preschool handles birthdays. Is morning or afternoon snack a better time? Any conflicts with field trips? What snacks make the biggest hit? Sometimes a child is given special privileges for the day—he is the one to pick the story read at rest time, to lead the line to the playground, to pick the color of the play dough the class is making, even wear a Happy Birthday name tag.

In fact, child care may make enough of a fuss for you to avoid the chaos of giving a birthday party yourself—which is fine, if you choose. You may have another party on the weekend, but child care friends are important too. There are plenty of years ahead of you to fuss, and even the treat at child care is often hard for three- and four-year-olds to handle. Tears before, during, and after are not uncommon.

Holidays like Valentine's Day and Halloween, the Fourth of July, Thanksgiving, and Presidents' Day are opportunities for art projects and for dressing up. To three- and four-year-olds, a week can seem as long as a month, and special days break the monotony. They help a child to begin organizing the year. The names of the months may be hard to keep straight, but everybody knows that Valentine's Day comes before St. Patrick's Day and Halloween before Thanksgiving.

The next area is more sensitive—religious holidays. If your child is in child care in your church or temple, holidays will of course be celebrated according to your beliefs. In other centers, however, religious holidays will be celebrated like St. Patrick's Day and Halloween. That is, Christmas carols are more likely to be "Jingle Bells" and "Santa Claus Is Coming to Town" than "Away in a Manger"; Easter probably will focus on dyeing eggs and bunnies rather than Resurrection.

This essentially leaves you with two choices. If you make yourself familiar with what your caregiver is doing to mark a holiday, you can then take pains to keep that aspect in perspective. You might ask if the director would like you to share your holiday's meaning with your child's class. Or—and we don't say this lightly —you may decide that you want your child in a form of child care that shares your own approach.

Despite the fact that they aren't involved in religious doctrine, caregivers are very concerned with right and wrong and honesty. They rely on the model of good citizenship. Many day-care mothers and centers will teach children the Pledge of Allegiance (try to make time to hear a group of three-year-olds pledging to "one nation, under God, indibidible"); some might even tackle "The Star-Spangled Banner." What people do and don't do is based on honesty and truth ("That is not your car. That is Billy's car.") and on respect ("We don't hit people. That hurts.")

All of these issues are complicated ones. Deciding how you feel about them and how you want them handled will take time and thought, discussion between parents, and between parents and caregiver. They are not jarring on a day-to-day basis as some of the issues we discussed in Part Two can be, but they sometimes cast longer shadows. Deciding to live with your caregiver's choices of menus and naptime may mean changing your schedule, but debating how you want your child taught right and wrong is a far different thing. If you decide that your caregiver's emphasis on citizenship is a good enough foundation, you are also implicitly accepting the responsibility for religious training and explanations and for finding ways to fit the two world views together without confusing your child.

This may be a time when you want to look around to see if there are centers whose views more nearly echo your own. It's one of the conflicts we'll be discussing in the next chapter.

C H A P T E R T W E L V E

PROBLEMS WITH A CAPITAL *P*

· ·

People d o n ' t l i k e to talk about a child care arrangement that goes sour. Superstition, perhaps—mentioning
the possibility might make it more likely to happen. But just as
you need to know which everyday frictions are inevitable and
must be lived with (as we discussed in Chapter 7), you also need to
know how to tell when a situation is breaking down, both from
your side and from the caregiver's. Causes on both sides range
from just plain unworkable situations to small problems that were
allowed to get out of hand. We're going to discuss them here in
hopes that you can effect a change from one kind of child care to
another with a minimum of heartache. Perhaps you can even work
your problems through once you see them clearly.

OUTGROWING YOUR CAREGIVER

Let's begin with one of the few positive reasons for changing child care—when your child has outgrown one form and needs to move on. Babysitting arrangements, however warm, rarely seem like enough once a baby is on her feet and on the go. Parents generally look around for play groups, then play groups that meet more frequently; by two-and-a-half or three, almost all children are in some kind of group care for some portion of the day. In fact, the numbers of children in child care put pressure on the others to join—one mother of five kept her first three at home till kindergarten, but by the time the last two arrived, preschool was the only place she could find playmates for them.

By sensing their child's need to be with other children, parents are responding in a healthy way to their children's needs. But they sometimes don't realize that caregivers respond too. Most nannies or sitters prefer babies. Much as you may want to keep the relationship going, your sitter may be ready to move on to younger charges she sees as less demanding and more fun.

You may be able to continue with your sitter by shifting to a part-time basis. Your child might go to a preschool in the mornings, coming home to the sitter in the afternoons. This is a particularly valuable arrangement if you have a second, younger child who you feel is better off with a sitter. Of course, it has its drawbacks too. The most obvious is the cost. The sitter will probably charge you a full rate since your child's presence for half a day prevents her from taking another full-time child. With the preschool as well, you are paying for two kinds of child care for one child.

A more serious drawback, however, is the difficulty we discussed in Chapter 10—getting everybody involved in your child's growth to pull in the same direction. It won't always be easy to

mesh your attitudes with a caregiver's; it is infinitely more complicated to find a fit with two different caregivers. If a child care
center does things differently than a sitter, most sitters are not
interested in changing their methods to match. That leaves you in
the thankless position of mediator. We don't mean that you
shouldn't try a part-time relationship, just to caution that it can
cause problems as well as solve them. But, even if you can't afford
this solution over the long term, use it for a transition period if
you can—keep your sitter for the first few weeks, even months
that your child is in group care. As well as making your child's
adjustment easier, it gives you something to fall back on if you
need it.

WHEN A SITTER RELATIONSHIP GOES SOUR

There are two other, less happy reasons why a sitter relationship
ceases to work, one from the parents' point of view and one from
the caregiver's point of view. The parent's again relates to their
child's age. At three and four, children begin to take on values, and
you want them to be your own. Qualities about your caregiver
that didn't concern you in your child's infancy make a difference
when you begin to see your caregiver as a potential role model.
Perhaps she always invited her friends over in the afternoon; you
knew and looked the other way. Now you mind. If she lives with
you, perhaps she entertains in her room. Now it worries you. You
knew she was a careless driver and handled it by not allowing her
to drive your car or take your child any place in hers. Now, when
your son watches her squeal out of the driveway on two wheels,
you wonder.

One woman praised her nanny's initiative—she took the children fishing, she took them ice skating. Then she found that the
nanny sneaked the children into the rink each time by pretending
that they were part of somebody else's birthday party. Another

found it funny when the housekeeper tried to get her son to stop crying by threatening to call the police, but when she realized that her son took it seriously, she did too. Every relationship contains differences, but when something tilts the balances and you are uncomfortable, it probably won't tilt back again. Rather, everything that happens will suddenly seem to underline your new, negative opinion.

The reason that in-home care goes sour from a caregiver's point of view is very different. Her employers add too many tasks that she believes she was not hired to do. Some adapting and renegotiating is inevitable. But if you are not tactful and if you don't try to see your caregiver's perspective, you may well lose her, even though she loves your children and is otherwise happy. And with her as with you, once the balance has tilted and she feels unappreciated, you are not likely to win her back again.

OUTGROWING GROUP CARE

A child's age can make parents aware of a poor fit in a group care situation as well. When a caregiver is both experienced and sensitive to the needs of your child, that will be all you need or want for the first eighteen months to two years. But as more and more conversations involve why people shouldn't do some things and should do others, you may gradually realize that, much as you like your caregiver and your child care setting, she's just not the role model you want now. When this happens with a sitter, you begin to disapprove of her, which makes severing the relationship a bit easier. But in group care, you may continue to like and respect the director and still feel that the program is too far from your own doctrinal beliefs.

Your views may change. People who have let church and temple attendance lapse during their single and young-married years often seem to rediscover their roots when their children are two or three.

If that happens to you, you may want your child's care to reflect your own renewed interests.

Other parents, by the way, make the same choice but move in the opposite direction. That is, parents in small neighborhood centers or church-sponsored ones may be happy for the first two years, then worry that their child is being taught beliefs they don't share. This varies tremendously from one part of the country to another, but many parents agree with the mother who said, "Preschool is really the last chance that parents have to choose what their kids are taught."

Finally, parents may become dissatisfied with their own level of involvement. As we pointed out in Chapter 2, parents want different kinds of involvement. You may not always realize that active participation matters to you until your child has been in care for a time. If you then discover that you want a part in the center's decision making, that may mean moving to a co-op center or one with a parent advisory board.

Most parents who feel dissatisfied, however, miss something very different. Parents too need nurturing—to feel that their views are listened to and their parenting respected. If you don't feel this from your caregiver, no matter how content and well cared for your child seems, you may want to look around for someone more responsive.

SERIOUS TROUBLE WITH OTHER CHILDREN

In the above situations, the child may be wholly unaware of what is making her parents uncomfortable. But now we come to a category of problems that arise from the child's discomfort. The first is trouble with other children.

Biting is probably the first instance of it. Whether their child is the biter or the bitten, some parents resolve this issue by withdrawing their child.

Let's be clear about this: Biting can be a serious problem *if* the caregiver is doing nothing about it. If there is a pattern of biting in your daughter's group, whether she is the biter or the bitten, you need to be reassured that your caregiver is watching and trying to change the situation in the many ways we discussed earlier. If she simply shrugs and plans to wait it out, you are indeed being given an ominous signal.

Often the phase passes and with closer supervision and redirection the biter's frustration (and thus the biting) is reduced. Sometimes a short respite from care is useful for all concerned. If the director has not been helpful, use the time to find a center with a more responsive director.

Older children may also have problems with others, as we discussed in Chapter 10. Some are aggressive; others always seem to be the victims of bullying by other children. As with biting, these are definitely problems with a capital *P*, and not every caregiver will handle them wisely. For example, one three-year-old girl who was all smiles toward her new baby brother became very aggressive with the children in her preschool group. Her mother, who had no trouble seeing the connection, was taken aback when the preschool director failed to see the child's unhappiness, responding instead with heavy discipline. After the parents talked it over with each other and their pediatrician, they moved their child. "I happened to have good insight into that one," said the mother, "but what if she was equally shortsighted about something I knew nothing about? You have to be able to trust somebody." The guidance we've described in Chapter 10 will give you an idea of what you have a right to expect, either from your present caregiver or from the new places that you interview.

While you want to be sure that overly aggressive or passive behavior is handled wisely, moving your child out of group care altogether is not always a good solution. After all, a child has to learn how to live in a group, and you don't want either victim or bully to become a child's permanent picture of herself. A sitter may unconsciously encourage aggressive behavior by taking the side of your child against her playmates; she may shelter a passive child, thus reinforcing the child's image of herself as weak.

SEXUAL EXPERIMENTATION AND ABUSE

Aggressive or passive behavior, while not a sign of a satisfied child, is nevertheless well within a child's normal range. Sometimes parents come across behavior that is not. Bathroom talk and curiosity about the differences between boys and girls, for example, are to be expected during the third and fourth years. Sometimes, though, a parent uncomfortably concludes that a child is showing curiosity and knowledge and exotic vocabulary beyond the normal. What's the guideline and how do you handle it?

People in the field say that you can make a rough division between what children are born knowing and what they must learn, either by watching or being touched or told. Babies know that the genital area is well endowed with nerve endings that make touch pleasant; thus infantile masturbation is an instinctive behavior. Oral sex play, on the other hand, probably won't occur to a three- or four-year-old; it has to be learned. That's the kind of knowledge that signals you that something undesirable is happening somewhere in your child's life. If your daughter wants to know what happens when a boy "kisses another boy *there*" or uses some other labored and circuitous wording to ask the same question, it probably means that she has either watched oral sex play or been told about it, and that should set up a scream from every alarm system you've got.

An incident like this is fortunately rare—a recent national study found that children in licensed child care facilities were at lower risk of sexual abuse than in their own homes. But you nevertheless need to know what to do if it occurs. If you have a conversation like this with your child, you must talk to your caregiver immediately, even if it involves taking time off from work. The odds are overwhelming that another child rather than a caregiver is involved. What generally happens is that a child talks about or acts out at the center behavior she has seen at home.

When you speak to your caregiver, you may find that she is already aware of the problem. But you need that reassurance from her, you need it in detail, and you need it on the spot.

Here's the process she should describe to you: When a caregiver thinks she observes overly precocious sexual behavior, she first observes till she knows who initiated it rather than who is imitating it. (In a center, teachers and director may both observe to make sure that they are on firm ground when they talk to the parents.) She must then talk to the child's parents immediately to find out how the knowledge came about. If it happens a second time, she will suggest some form of family counseling (either she will have names or she will send the family to a social service agency or to a pediatrician).

If the name of an adult comes up, the issue may no longer be sex play between children but alleged child abuse. This is also true if you see any physical signs that your child may have been abused. Pain or difficulty with urination is always a reason to seek a doctor's help. It may be a symptom of a bladder infection (which requires prompt treatment), but if the doctor observes swelling, bruising, or bleeding in the genital area, physical abuse may be indicated.

In a case of alleged child abuse, a center director is required by state law to inform the appropriate social service agency (as is a doctor). She will cooperate with a counselor or social agency representative as requested. Depending on the state, police or law-enforcement agencies may become involved as well.

The caregiver should assure you that she is in some stage of that process and is downplaying the incident with the children to avoid giving it undue importance until the investigation is completed.

Your next question is how is she handling the issue with the children and how should you handle it at home. If the problem appears to be sex play between children, she is probably redirecting the children's attention when conversation or behavior occurs—and meanwhile keeping an eagle eye on the child who is having the problems. She will recommend that you try to be equally low-key at home. Shock, disbelief, or disgust will lead a child to feel very guilty.

It's a good idea to talk to children without waiting for an incident. Some centers plan regular programs—Kinder-Care works with caregivers, parents, and children. With the help of film character Dolly the Dog, children as young as two-and-a-half learn to say, "No, no, I do not go/With anyone I do not know." They learn when touching is and is not acceptable, how to turn away an inappropriate question or gesture, and the importance of talking to teachers and parents if something happens.

What happens if you don't get a satisfactory response from your child's caregiver? Is there somebody higher up you could talk to? A supervisor or owner of a center, perhaps a supervising agency for a day-care mother? You might want to consult with the appropriate state agency. A lack of interest is rare, however.

If the problem turns out to be more than sex play between children, confidentiality takes over, and the caregiver generally won't discuss the situation beyond telling you that it has been turned over to a state agency. When a sexual abuse problem involves an adult rather than another child, the setting is most often a casual arrangement—babysitters, family members, an unlicensed day-care mother. This is one of the reasons we so strongly recommend that you seek *licensed* care. In many states, teachers at a licensed center have had a background check for sex offenses. In a center, the building design protects children too. There are few walls extending all the way up to the ceiling, few closed spaces—even the bathroom doors are open—and adults constantly oversee one another.

A child's accusation, by the way, isn't automatic proof that an adult is involved. She may be trying to shield another child or a parent; she may have an imperfect understanding of what she is saying and no idea of how damaging her exciting story can be. If you and your spouse both feel that the situation is not being handled properly, though, take your child out of the setting immediately and report your concerns to a hot line or Protective Services (within the Human Resources Department of your state government). If you're wrong, you've just caused yourself some inconvenience. Your child doesn't have the time for you to wait to see if you're right.

Fortunately, this situation is rare. You will almost certainly not be faced with it, but it's important to be informed and to know the proper agency to work with in case of suspicion and concern.

ONE ILLNESS AFTER ANOTHER

Another problem that involves other children is not behavior but illness. There will probably be periods in every family's life with child care when illness becomes a problem with a capital *P*. Any illness, even when it's not a lengthy one like measles or chicken pox, throws the whole family instantly into crisis mode. Even if company rules permit you to take your own sick days to care for your child, the demands of your own job may make it difficult to use the time as often as you need to. A caregiver doing her job properly is going to call you if your child has a temperature over a hundred, asking you to come to pick up your child. How often can you get up and walk out on such short notice? Perhaps husband and wife can share the burden; perhaps a grandmother can help (but most likely she's working too).

In Chapter 8 we talk about how to cover for a child's illness. Here we want to talk about what happens when one illness begins to run into the next. A cold makes the rounds, and just as the hacking coughs finally quiet, somebody new begins to sniffle.

When you walk your child into the day-care home in the morning, it seems that half the children there have that dull-eyed, transparent look that means they are coming down with something.

Rounds of illness are a problem for parent and caregiver alike. Usually there's no single cause but rather several small problems adding up to a big one. If it's happening to you, begin by going over some sanitation basics with your caregiver. (At a center, you would speak to the director, who would speak to the teachers.) Does she wash her hands each time she changes an infant? Is she using lots of soap and scrubbing hard? Does she wash off the snack table both before and after snack? Do the children wash their hands often, again with lots of soap and scrubbing?

Review, too, the conditions for which children should stay home. State regulations for child care centers offer some guidelines. Diarrhea can be one of the worst problems in group care. It is usually so contagious that even if the sick child is withdrawn immediately, there may be three or four more cases before the center has it under control. After repeated bouts, a concerned mother will have her child's stool tested; if no virus is present, the child may be readmitted. If diarrhea is making the rounds at your child's center or day-care home, maybe you should suggest that the caregiver use disposable gloves while changing diapers.

Some conditions for which children must be immediately withdrawn and not readmitted till seen by a doctor include: a temperature of over 100 degrees, any type of vomiting, pinkeye, and ear infections. If a child has an infection that needs to be treated with an antibiotic, she must usually stay out for at least twenty-four hours, though this rule varies with the physician. Then there are the biggies: measles, chicken pox, strep throat. When a case is present, your caregiver should warn all the other parents; if the next child with a scratchy throat is tested for strep immediately and kept home from the very beginning, perhaps the cycle of illness can be broken.

These regulations are sound. The problem doesn't really lie in them but in the fact that parents stretch them. The day after a child has been sent home sick, some parents, unable to miss work, fill her full of acetaminophen to keep her fever down and send her in again. Or when the caregiver calls a parent at work to pick up a sick child, she discovers that he has changed jobs without notifying the center so the telephone number no longer applies, or the parent is about to go into a meeting (which is probably why that child was brought in sick in the first place) and can't get free for several hours. During the intervening hours, even if the sick child can be separated from others (as in the director's office of a center or a sick child area), she can't be given medication, and she needs a parent or family member.

That kind of neglect—and it is neglect—is unfair to a child who is already miserable, and it will probably make the oncoming illness more serious. Occasionally, it can be dangerous. The H-flu meningitis that spikes a harmless 100-degree fever at ten o'clock may be 104 by two o'clock and a coma by the end of the day. Occasionally, too, a parent will respond to an illness call this carelessly not once but many times. A center director may even call a social worker to talk to him or her.

But a far more common problem is a simpler one: In group child care, if each family stretches the rules just a bit, just now and then, the result is a constant round of illness for all. Thus you really need the cooperation of every other parent. Ask your caregiver if she would consider an evening meeting at which a pediatrician could talk to all the parents about recognizing the signs of illness and the consequences of ignoring them.

At the same meeting, discuss the importance of an emergency back-up. If every parent knows that an aunt or grandparent or neighbor will pick up a child in an emergency, each parent is more willing to make the arrangement him/herself. If every parent has some way to cover for a sick child, it becomes easier to keep your own child home. Since parents who go to the same sitter or day-care home or center tend to live in the same area, maybe you can compare back-up names and offer some sitter suggestions to the parents whose children are most ill most often.

WHEN YOU'VE BEEN ASKED TO LEAVE

The final area of problems are small problems that get out of hand, usually involving payment or schedules. In Chapter 7, we talked about both—about how important it is to be prompt, both with picking up your child and with paying—and how unfortunate it can be to have a good situation deteriorate because you haven't followed through. Here we'll talk about what happens when the situation has gone too far to be put right.

A family day-care mother or a child care center will give you very clear signals. There are fines for lateness; you'll be given a few warnings; then, at the discretion of the day-care mother or center director, you'll be asked to withdraw your child. With a sitter or nanny or housekeeper, the handwriting won't appear on the wall quite so clearly. Sometimes she'll ask for time off when a member of the family is visiting and she just won't come back. Or her sick days will increase. Or you will see your child get ever more cranky and sullen and clinging.

Being asked to leave a child care setting—or knowing that something you've done has made the situation unworkable—is very like being fired. You'll feel uncomfortable and guilty and desperate. That's not a good mindset in which to look for a replacement.

Before you even begin to look, then, take the time to examine the reasons why you couldn't handle either payment or schedules. The reason is usually painfully simple: You have less control of your life than you thought you did. You picked a child care setting a little more expensive than you could really afford, hoping you could pare down your other expenses. But you couldn't. Or you picked a setting that offered fewer hours than you really needed, hoping you'd always be able to slide for bases. But you couldn't.

Next time be more realistic about money and/or time. When you get the coverage you really need for what you really can pay, you're going to find it possible to do your share just as well as anybody else, and this episode will be history.

CHANGING CHILD CARE SETTINGS

It is neither fun nor easy to move from one child care situation to another. No matter how poorly the situation may be working now, it must have good qualities as well, or you wouldn't have chosen it in the first place. As we've shown, often the parents are the ones who see shortcomings; the children cling to what they know, not realizing that something better can be found. Manners seem to play a part. Although once you've withdrawn your child, you need never see the caregiver again, you may be afraid of hurting her feelings or of the criticisms she might make of you in return. You want to be fair about giving notice to a housekeeper— yet once you've made your dissatisfaction formal and final, how will she treat your child in the days that she's working out her notice?

Logistics are no fun either. Ideally, you'd have your next child care setting picked out before you let go of this one and make the transfer with the minimum of fuss. In real life, you probably won't be that lucky. One woman who had put ads with a carefully anonymous post office box number in the local papers got a reply from her present housekeeper! If you don't have an alternative ready, we recommend that you plan for a gap of two to three weeks between one situation and the next, using temporary care to bridge the gap. If you take away the pressure for an instant solution, you can take the time to find a setting that works.

One final note: As you look and interview, human nature will make you concentrate on what went wrong the last time. That is, if illness was a problem, you'll want a center that looks like a surgery. If you thought the children were too aggressive, this time you'll feel reassured by a circle of blank smiling nebbishes. Listen to your child. What does she miss? You want to repeat what worked as well as to avoid what didn't.

PART FOUR

SPOTLIGHT ON YOU

By n o w y o u should have a clear picture of the different kinds of child care and how each will change a child's life, on through day-to-day routines and the ways in which many of the events of childhood are handled. Now it's your turn: In Part Four, we turn the spotlight on *your* life.

You probably thought that when your child was in child care, you could (and should) keep that part of your life tucked firmly away from your workday. Not so. Having a child in child care, even good care, affects the routines of your work life much as the routines of child care affect your child's life. In Chapter 13, we'll tell you how. We'll talk about the changes you'll adapt to—and even come to think positively about—and how to minimize the changes that can be definite drawbacks.

. . . .

Having a child in child care influences your life in other ways as well. There are effects on your parenting. What happens to family life? What happens to your feelings about yourself as a parent, and your *child*'s feelings about you as a parent, when you spend so much time apart? How do women respond? How do men? In Chapter 14, we'll talk about these feelings and about how to use your evenings and weekends so positively that your doubts fade.

Then there are the other people in your life: spouse, family, friends. They play different roles in the lives of working families than in the Mommy-at-home family of the fifties. Then, the people in your life relieved boredom and varied the routine. Today, some kinds of relationships add laughter and confidence to your life—not to mention helping to keep your head above water—while others threaten to drown you. How do you find and nurture good ones and recognize and avoid the others? See Chapter 15.

Finally, in Chapter 16 we'll wrap up the whole life-style of child care while you work: what child care can be, and because of it, what your family is free to be.

CHAPTER THIRTEEN

NINE TO FIVE:

How Child Care Affects Your Work
· · · · · · · · · · · · · · · · · · ·

There is no question that being a parent—and thus living with child care—will affect you as a working person. Before you start wringing your hands, though, look at this list of other things wholly unrelated to child care that can also affect the workday:

- Being single and going out eight nights a week

- Being newly separated and crying yourself to sleep eight nights a week

- Looking for an apartment at a rent you can afford

- Living in Chicago and trying to carry on a love affair with somebody in San Francisco

- Daily visits to a parent who is critically ill

- Having (and trying to hide) an affair with the head of your department

- Going to school at night for your MBA

All your co-workers, in other words, have other interests in life besides work, sometimes happy, sometimes stressful. The only difference is that for you the happy/stressful component at the moment happens to be parenthood.

Remember this the next time you are lured by the Working Mother's Lament ("If Only I Were at Home I'd Be a Perfect Mother"). Certainly there are many aspects of working and having children that are worth feeling guilty about, and we're going to talk about them. But it's one thing to feel guilty about specific ways in which you are coping poorly and could learn to do better. An automatic conviction that quitting work would solve all your problems is something very different. (It would certainly replace some problems with others, but that's not always a satisfactory solution.) We call that *knee-jerk guilt,* and we want you to learn to keep it in perspective. You'll probably never be entirely rid of it, but you can learn to recognize its irrationality and turn your back on it.

As we talk about the effects of child care on work—which are very real and sometimes daunting—we want to make you aware of three things. First, there are ways you may be able to make your workdays smoother. Second, and perhaps more important, you should alert yourself to the role knee-jerk guilt plays throughout —that is, the ways in which people in your work world (including you) try to make you feel ashamed for subjecting your family to this juggling act instead of helping you to take it in stride. And third, you need to know the ways your company can and should support you.

People concerned about combining children and work have one advantage over people with the other problems listed at the beginning of this chapter. Unlike them, your problems have been studied in exhaustive detail. Businesses like AT & T, business organizations like the Conference Board, magazines, prominent educators like Ellen Galinsky, the Department of Labor—all have gotten into the act, and their findings have been remarkably consistent. The problems and feelings you are likely to experience are shared by just about all the other working parents in this country.

Your work will be affected in several ways. One is lateness. Getting to work on time, staying at your desk every minute of the day—you don't have the same control over either that you once did. Another is the time you spend at work dealing with child care. When you call to remind your caregiver to take your child to the playground or to make arrangements for a playmate; when your caregiver calls about problems with your child or an overflowing washing machine or supplies you've run out of; when you sit at your desk staring into space, worrying about being away from your baby for three days next week on a trip you can't (and don't want to) miss—all this takes time away from a job you are being paid to do. Still another is emergencies. He's at the center with a fever of 101 and you have to pick him up within the hour; he has diarrhea and can't go back to the day-care mother's without a pediatrician's note (and the pediatrician doesn't have evening hours); your sitter has decided to quit without giving any notice; your child's center has a holiday and your office doesn't. Finally, there are all the ways your company can support (or interfere with) your needs as a parent.

Let's look at these one at a time.

GETTING TO WORK LATE AND LEAVING EARLY

Studies of various companies show that forty to seventy percent of the work force comes late or leaves early sometime within any three-month period because of child care concerns. Allowing for executives who don't clock in and out and for studies that rely on their respondents' word (the lie factor), it's safe to assume that everybody has trouble sticking to their official office hours day in and day out. Women are about twice as apt to have problems as men. The younger the children, and the more children, the more apt people are to have to come late or leave early.

Studies have also explored the relationship of different kinds of child care to lateness. People with out-of-home care are more apt to have trouble than people with in-home care. And, most significant of all, the people who are having problems with child care are the most apt to come late and leave early.

If twice as many women are having problems, it's reasonable to conclude that twice as many women are dropping off and picking up their children from child care or lingering to give last-minute instructions to the sitter. It's obvious, then, that most men and women don't divide their parenting chores evenly.

That obvious imbalance, however, doesn't mean that change will be equally obvious to map out or to bring about. In most two-job households, the man is still considered the major bread-winner, even if the family would sink without the woman's income. That feeling goes very deep. Shake your husband awake some morning at three A.M. and whisper, "Whose job matters more, yours or mine?" and in the helpless honesty of half-sleep, we guarantee he'll answer, "Mine."

Will that still be true in ten years' time? We don't have time to worry about it—and we doubt that you do either. We doubt, too, that you have mental or emotional or physical time for a big ideological argument about what's fair.

Get at the problem another way. Which of you has more control over the structure of his/her job? In other words, can you (can he) schedule meetings after ten in the morning or before four in the afternoon? Can you (can he) organize the first or last hour for the kind of catch-up correspondence that has no particular deadline, or that can be done equally well at home or during the lunch hour? That's the person who can most conveniently drop off and pick up a child from child care or give instructions to a sitter.

Which of you is most dependent on a boss? Which of you has a job that requires you to fit in to somebody else's schedule? Depending on the boss, that person is *least* able to drop off or pick up.

In other words, the determining factor should be whose job is more flexible, not whose parenting assignment it has always been. The equation between the two of you is a personal one. No outsider can tell you what the balance should be. But we can tell you to check it from time to time to see if it's still a fair one.

You may be able to make more effective use of child care too. If your center provides breakfast and you aren't signed up for it, that might buy you a half hour every morning. If it does not offer breakfast now, suggest it. This is an increasingly common request, one to which a center may well listen. Or scout around for a center that provides it. If a center or day-care mother provides lunch, you save the minutes spent packing lunch each morning. There may be centers in your area that are open for an hour or two longer than the one your child is in now. Never assume that the cost will automatically be higher than you now pay until you check it out. Centers in any given area try very hard to keep their rates competitive even when their services vary.

You may need to add a caregiver to your schedule—a neighbor who will care for your child for an hour each morning and take her to the center or pick her up in the evening. Perhaps another mother at the center can cover for you in the morning, while you cover for her in the evening.

In other words, child care really can work for you. What gets in the way for most parents is knee-jerk guilt. Try substituting one of the other problems we listed in the beginning of this chapter and you'll realize what we mean. If you were an hour late some morning because you had the chance to look at a super apartment, would you slink into the office flushed and sweating, hoping no one saw you and apologizing if they did? Nonsense. You'd come in openly, bubbling over with your find and describing it to everybody, and you'd expect your co-workers to share or, at least respect, your excitement. If you went to the dentist you'd come in mumbling with a lopsided smile and expect sympathy. But we don't give ourselves the same break when we are late because of a child care mishap, even though it probably occurs no more often.

That's partly your problem, partly that of your co-workers. We don't know how re-educable they are, but you can certainly change your own attitude. See to it that you keep other reasons for lateness under control—there are dentists who work on Saturdays, and you may have to do apartment hunting then too, even if you have to pass up something wonderful. Once you have employed all the strategies we've discussed here, give yourself credit for having done all you can and make peace with the fact that even with all your planning, you'll still occasionally be late. If your boss isn't reasonable about it, do what one woman does: She keeps a running list of other people's excuses that her boss *does* accept and uses them instead.

DEALING WITH CHILD CARE ON THE JOB

The percentage of workers on the phone at three-thirty P.M. is probably higher than at any other time of day—and they are not all talking to clients. They are doing an after-school check on their kids. Studies show that employers are well aware of it, and employees readily admit to it. Employers estimate that two thirds to three quarters of their employees lose time to coping with child care problems on the job. In one study, a quarter to a half of workers say they are worrying about their children almost all the time they are at work.

Your first reaction to those statistics is undoubtedly relief—you're not alone—followed by guilt. It looks as though working parents never give their companies a fair shake.

But when we looked closer at the studies, we found a few other findings which we think suggest ways to get this problem too under control. The first is this: Of people who consider that they have few or no child care problems, *over half* nevertheless deal with child care issues on the job. When people are unhappy with their child care, the figure shoots up to seventy-seven percent for men, and ninety-four percent for women.

That finding is suggestive in two very different ways. The first and most obvious: Satisfaction with your child care will cut down on its intrusion into your work life. Getting and keeping good child care is fair to your employer as well as to you and your child.

The second and equally important point: Even when things are going well, you will still think about child care while you are working. We are, in other words, talking about two things here—child care *issues* and child care *problems*. The purpose of this book is to help you outwit the problems. Once you've done so, however, the issues will remain. Everybody has to deal with them. Everybody has to talk to his or her sitter or center director, make appointments with the pediatrician, and track down birthday party favors, and some of those things can best be done between nine and five. This fact will always be with you.

So how do you deal with it?

First, if you hang your head in shame at the thought of having anything to do with child care while you're at work, how much of your reaction is knee-jerk guilt? Look around at your co-workers: They make appointments to have their cars inspected or have their hair done, make lunch dates, call travel agents—all without guilt. They consider that part of a normal life. *Children are too.*

As with lateness, don't pile child care concerns on top of car inspections and calls to the travel agent. For you, child care fills up the category of things allowed to intrude on your work life, and the other things must either be handled by your spouse or on evenings and weekends.

Presentation matters here too. Try to confine phone calls to certain times of the day, and pick times that are least intrusive into the routines of other people, particularly your boss. Think of this time as your coffee break. Once you define it that way to yourself, you'll have little trouble saying so, matter-of-factly rather than shamefacedly, to others.

That attitude can make more of a difference than you realize. If your boss walks in during a call and you look up and say calmly, "This is the time I check in with the sitter. Be with you in a minute," you convey that the situation is under control. On the other hand, if you flush, mumble a disjointed apology and hang up in midsentence, along with the obvious guilt, your message is that your life is disorganized. Whatever he says, your boss doesn't really care that you deal with child care concerns at the office. His fears are (1) that those concerns will swallow up your workday, and (2) that you are helpless to prevent it. Demonstrate that you are in control and you will also be reassuring him that your children don't interfere with your job.

MISSING WORK BECAUSE OF CHILD CARE

Three child care problems cause people to miss the most work—problems finding child care, breakdowns in care, and caring for sick children. If you missed at least one day in the past three months because of any of them, you're about average. One study done in New York came up with a much higher figure—one day every three *weeks.*

Absences show the same division between men and women that tardiness does. Women miss about twice as many workdays as men. Age of children is a factor too. Women with children under school age miss about twice as many workdays as those with children in first grade or older. Women's higher rates reflect the fact that they are considered the parent in charge of child care—and that in turn happens because their job is considered less demanding. When both men and women have less demanding, low-paying jobs, both men and women have more absences.

Once again, let's separate what you can change and what you cannot. Go over the reasons why you cover for problems twice as often as your husband does. Is it because he has a more responsible job? That may indeed make it harder for him to be away from his desk—but it's just as likely that it makes it easier for him to say, "I'll work on this report at home tomorrow. See you Thursday morning." Conversely, having a less responsible job may make it harder to get away—if you are a hairdresser or a waitress, your income depends on being there. If you're a secretary, your boss doesn't function as well when you're not there and will resent your absence. Do you take charge simply out of habit? Habits can be changed.

The quality of your child care plays a role here too. If you have good care, you're less apt to need time to search for new care or to cover for the abrupt departure of a caregiver. Since good child care tends to be safer and cleaner, you may also indirectly cut down on the number of illnesses your child has.

But, even in the best of circumstances, you'll have to face the fact of many childhood illnesses. The exception is in-home care. If you don't have in-home care, a child's illness represents not only worry but the unwelcome added expense of a last-minute sitter. Once again we stress how essential it is to have back-up help set up in advance—either relatives, friends, or neighbors for whom you can trade weekend babysitting for their help during your child's illness.

As we have said elsewhere, a child's illness is one of the times when we feel parents should make every effort to be there. It won't always be possible. But it should *sometimes* be possible, and you should feel no guilt about taking days off to care for a sick child. A recent nationwide survey found that most parents do so and don't consider it a problem.

Some companies acknowledge this right openly by a policy of allowing employees to use their own sick days to care for their children. (It's a self-serving policy. One day spent when a child is mildly ill may get him back on his feet again; without that day, he may become so ill that his parents catch it as well, causing much more lost work time in the end.) Others allow employees to use personal time. A few companies even keep a visiting nurse on the payroll to care for the sick children of employees. (This sounds terrific on paper. In real life, illnesses like flu and chicken pox tend to come in bunches and a nurse is either not needed at all or needed in half a dozen places at once.)

HOW A GOOD COMPANY CAN MAKE YOUR LIFE EASIER

Whether the issue is lateness, time spent at work dealing with child care, or emergencies, (two characteristics always seem to remain constant.) The first is that there *will be* some effects, which you can minimize and control but not eliminate. The second is that these effects need not interfere with how well you do your job. If you have done all you can to minimize lateness and plan ahead for sick days and your company still makes you feel apologetic about being a parent, then the time may have come for you to look for a job that fits your family's needs better.

This is what we think of as the fourth effect of child care on work—looking for a job that suits your family better—and on the other side, enlightened companies actively using job benefits to recruit new people. This isn't a daydream. You are going to have your children for a long time. You need the best working conditions you can find, and companies throughout the country are learning that helping with child care makes it easier to find and keep employees. (Merck Pharmaceuticals, Nyloncraft in Indiana, and Intermedics in Texas are examples of companies progressive in this regard.) In one nationwide survey, twenty-five percent of the women and even more men had refused a new job or promotion or transfer that they felt would entail less time for their families. One man in five and one woman in four had changed jobs in order to find one whose demands fit their families better. People are looking at their jobs with new eyes and when necessary voting with their feet.

What kind of help do you have the right to expect?

An understanding attitude toward maternity leave, for starters. Six months may be an ideal, but the reality is more like six to twelve weeks. That gives a woman time to recover from labor, gives the parents time to adapt to their new routines and to become acquainted with their infant, as well as time for all to find and adapt to child care. It gives the baby time to grow from a newborn of petallike fragility to a vigorous little person. This last is important to your peace of mind if you are a member of the majority that can't find or afford in-home care. You're overwhelmingly concerned with the safety of a newborn; she looks as though she might break. By the time she's a few months old, you can see that boredom is an equally important concern. And boredom may be the mother's concern as well by then—after three months, most women miss office friendships, routines, and challenges.

Maternal leave policy is just the beginning. Employers' involvement with working parents and child care grows daily—not in a tidy way but in a hodge-podge as complicated as the needs of their employees. Some companies help with the search for child care, for example. Many large companies help employees determine what they need through Employee Assistance Programs (EAP). Usually the program includes a consultant, whose services include occasional workshops to help parents determine their needs. The consultant may work with an agency in the area (and the company may pay the agency fees) that will help employees find the most suitable kind of care, from in-home to family day care to centers. The agency may even do follow-up interviews. (Check to be sure that the agency covers *all* the child care in your area. Some agencies don't make referrals to for-profit centers. Family day-care mothers or nannies may be registered with one agency but not with all. You want to choose from the broadest possible spectrum.)

Companies may help their employees pay for child care. A child care grant may be part of a cafeteria benefit plan, or the company may arrange for an employee to pay a certain percent of pretax income to be paid into an account earmarked for child care; his or her remaining income is then taxed at a lower rate. (Both of these approaches leave employees free to use the child care in their own neighborhoods.) In exchange for a guarantee that employees will use a center, a company may negotiate a lower fee for them or pay part of the fee (commonly about twenty percent). Sharing with the community in these ways may qualify a center for certain government grants, which in turn help keep costs down. About a hundred and twenty corporations nationwide (including Wang, Campbell Soup, Champion International, CIGNA, Walt Disney World and Stride Rite Shoes) have on-site child care for their employees, sometimes including the community.

Finally, companies can support you by helping you function day to day. Some companies do so by making working days more manageable through flexible working hours.

Flexible working hours most often mean that people work the same number of hours but on different schedules—beginning at seven A.M. and leaving at three instead of nine to five. Or beginning at eleven A.M., running till seven. Usually called Flextime, this work pattern makes it possible for two working parents to take their kids to doctor and dentist appointments, to drop off and pick up without panic, to share care for a sick child, even to pay for fewer hours and a higher quality of care. (Of course, it also limits the time they have together.)

Many companies also offer part-time work schedules—sixty percent of the companies recently surveyed by New York's Conference Board. Most often, though, part-time work is seen by companies as temporary—a way for women to ease back into the workplace after maternity leave or for special situations like caring for a child with a long-term illness or a disability.

One of the intriguing things about both Employee Assistance Programs (EAP) and flexible hours is that people don't value either one very highly unless they've had the chance to use it. If they *haven't* made use of flexible work time or EAP, employees put them at the bottom of the benefits they'd like. Those who have tried either, though, put them at the top of the list. In one Midwestern study, the more flexible workers' hours were, the more flexible they wanted to make them.

Finally, companies can provide you with an understanding boss. The least sympathetic boss we came across was a man who refused to let a woman take time off to be at the hospital while her son had his appendix out—using as his excuse the fact that *he* hadn't missed an hour at work when his son had open-heart surgery.

Things really are better these days. That boss probably couldn't get away with his attitude today—either his company would have more flexible policies or his wife would be working and would insist on his help. In one survey, about two-thirds of the employees throughout the country felt that their bosses were understanding about the time they needed to tend to family matters.

Unfortunately, that means you still have a one in three chance of working for a dragon. And dragons come in more than one guise. There are men like the example above—older, with wives who never worked, used to a sharp division between what men do and what women do. Their numbers are dwindling; they're retiring from the work force or being reeducated by wives and daughters. Then there are older women who made their career mark at a time when they either had to forgo children or purge all signs of them from their work life. These women can be startlingly resentful of younger women who want a more balanced life. Their attitude is, I made the sacrifices, why can't you? Finally, there are bosses whose lives parallel your own—either men or women who are part of a two-career marriage and know exactly how delicate your balancing act is because they have one too. Any problem you have that affects your work can look like one too many things for them in turn to juggle.

On a practical level, a boss who doesn't understand or sympathize with your needs can make it difficult for you to handle family issues as you need to. According to one study, your boss's attitude spills over into your image of yourself as a parent as well. New mothers with unsympathetic bosses felt they were less competent mothers as well as workers. The bosses' attitudes played as big a role in the amount of stress they felt as their husbands' did. Workers who have stress-related physical problems like shortness of breath and irregular heartbeat are apt to have two other things as well—breakdowns in child care and unsupportive bosses.

If you are interviewing, you can ask if a company considers it important for their managers to be sensitive to employees' needs, but you will probably have to feel his or her attitude out for yourself in the job interview. We recommend that you be upfront about the kind of understanding you want—not exaggerated but realistic. If you sound on top of your life, potential employers are quick to assume that you are on top of your abilities too.

A good leave policy, help in finding child care and financing it, support for handling its effects on your workday, a supportive boss —you deserve them all. For the sake of every part of your life, you need a work atmosphere that allows you to see child care issues as they really are—a normal part of your workday, not one that you abuse but not one that you neglect. *Everybody* needs that, and the more people insist upon it, the sooner it will be common policy for us all.

There is one final characteristic of people who must deal with child care issues on the job. Studies show that these people—which is to say, all of us—feel exhausted, rushed off their feet, impatient, and sometimes irritable.

And that's the person who's supposed to walk through the door each night and turn into Superparent. A challenging task. We'll show you how to pull it off in the next chapter.

CHAPTER FOURTEEN

THE SUCCESSFUL
REST-OF-THE-WEEK PARENT

· ·

Let's look at the parent who picks up her child from care each night. Studies can draw for us a pretty clear picture of the way she feels. Whether she likes her job or not, whether she likes her boss or not, by the end of the day she is tired. She is impatient and irritable, in no mood for any more problems. Above all, she is ready to go off duty.

Which is just what she can't do.

Everybody tells her—she tells herself—that she must find from somewhere new stores of energy and patience to do a presto change into another, equally demanding role: Quality-Time Parent. Ready to listen. Ready for fun. Ready for a nervous breakdown.

All too many working parents have expectations of themselves as workers, homemakers, and parents that just won't fit into the boundaries of a twenty-four-hour real-life day. So they set themselves up for failure day after day.

But believe it or not, there are many others who make the switch easily, who give every evidence of enjoying their evenings and weekends. What's their secret? They've learned how to parent under today's rules. That means that they've faced up to the nagging, unadmitted doubts all working parents share. And they've also learned to handle evenings and weekends in ways that relax and renew them.

That's what we're going to talk about here. First, we'll walk through the guilt and show you how guilt itself—not your job, not child care—can interfere with the kind of parenting and child care choices you make. And then we'll describe the happy ending —what evenings and weekends can be like when you don't feel compelled to fill them with high-compression parenting.

BLAMING YOUR JOB FOR PROBLEMS AT HOME

The knee-jerk guilt that makes you apologize for needing to handle child care issues at work comes home with you and does an aboutface. When you're at home, it's seductively simple to blame anything that goes wrong on the fact that you, an unnatural parent, are working. Then you've truly boxed yourself in. You couldn't win if you wanted to. Having a job means your priorities are wrong, that you are wasting your prime time and energy away from your child. Instead of saying, "I'm so tired," you tell yourself, "If I weren't working, I wouldn't be so tired." Not "What kind of fool dry cleaner closes at five-thirty?" but "If I weren't working, I could pick up the clothes during the day." We heard a sad version of this from a woman who had deliberately chosen *not* to work and to stay home with her children. When one of her teenagers got into serious trouble she cried out, "If only I were working, I'd have something to blame it on!"

It's fatally easy to make work a handy catchall for any failure to cope. The unhealthy corollary: Since you probably have little choice about working, you may assume you have no choice about the accompanying problems either.

That's not only wrong, it's dangerously wrong. Oh, you can live with permanently frazzled housekeeping, but what if somewhere down the road you have a more serious problem—which, given the nature of children, will almost certainly happen? Do you put that in the "guilt" box and give up on it too? Blaming your job for every glitch in your life can blind you to the reasons you have trouble coping and blind you as well to the possibility of change and of success.

Another common tendency is to blame yourself for not being there. She fell out of a tree and you weren't the one to take her to the emergency room. She learned her numbers, but not from you. She baked chocolate-chip cookies, but not with you. You're not there for emergencies or shared memories or milestones.

What are you afraid of, deep down? *Because you're not there, you're not acting like a parent.*

A *real* parent.

The question is, what kind of parent are you?

It is almost certainly true that you are not repeating the kind of parenting you had. Unfortunately, as one psychiatrist pointed out, no matter how good or bad their own parents were, working parents can fault themselves by comparison. If your mother was at home leading the Brownies and baking the brownies, you worry that you aren't doing as good a job for your child. But the opposite crops up frequently too, say family therapists. People whose mothers worked, now working parents themselves, worry about repeating the pattern. This is because a generation ago, the majority of women who worked were also divorced, scrambling to keep their family's head above water, often treated like social outcasts. If children felt singled out and insecure then, they are apt to associate their feelings with the stresses of a working parent rather than long outgrown attitudes toward divorce.

Even if you avoid guilt, though, you come up against the all-too-frequent feeling that as working parents you have few guidelines. How do you know whether you are doing a good job? If you take away polishing baby shoes and making your own baby food and being there to tuck your toddler in for his daily nap, what *is* a good job? Like it or not, you're pioneer parents, guinea pigs for your own grandchildren, forced to carve out and defend your definitions of working parenthood from one week to the next.

This concern goes beyond knee-jerk guilt. You need reassurance that is not easily found today. We're trying to help you define this new parenthood as we explain how you express your parenting through the caregiver you choose and how you work at parenting through and with your caregiver. In the next chapter, we'll talk about friends and groups who can help give you the confidence that once came from repeating what one's own parents had done. But you probably will never be entirely free of your feelings of uncertainty and isolation. Whenever something goes wrong, you're going to wonder what you could have done differently— what a "good" parent would or should have done. That doesn't mean you're not doing the best job you can—quite the contrary: That worry is part of doing the best job you can.

Then there's the fear of losing your child's love. Because you're not there, you're afraid your child won't get the chance to think of you as a parent and will become attached to your caregiver instead.

This concern too has a very real basis. Your child *is* going to fall in love with his sitter, or his day-care mother, or one of her children, or the center director, or one of his teachers, or the teacher he had last year, or (sensible child) the cook at his child care center. Or maybe all of them, along with his grandmothers and the Saint Bernard next door. Wholehearted, head-over-heels loving is one of the things small children do best.

A good sitter or day-care mother or center director will talk to you about this attachment when you interview. She'll explain that it is bound to happen, that it is healthy and desirable for your child to care for the people caring for him, and that he couldn't be open and loving if you as a parent hadn't done your job well.

On good days, you'll believe that. You'll watch your child hug his teacher passionately and say, Thank God. You tried to choose somebody he could care about; the fact that he does so reaffirms your decision and is therefore your success as well as his. On good days, you will be delighted to know that your child is spending his hours away from you happily.

When the washing machine has backed up, one of your child's sneakers is missing, your car has stalled three times in the rain, and you have to shop on the way home—those also seem to be the days when your child informs you that he has decided to call the sitter "Mommy."

A few years from now you'll look back and remember days like that, days when you understand down to your bone marrow how an oldest child feels when his mother brings home a squalling infant and has the nerve to say warmly, "I love you just as much as I ever did. There's room in my heart for two." But an occasional wave of jealousy, even hostility, doesn't mean you have bad child care or that you are a bad mother. It means you are having a rotten day. Or it may mean that your child has had a rotten day and knows that a dramatic plea to stay with his sitter instead of coming home will spoil your day too.

Parents also worry when they *don't* feel hostile and jealous, by the way. Many mothers welcome the attachment of their child to the caregiver, but they have been told so many stories about the jealousy they will feel that when they don't feel it, they wonder.

Along with bad days, you will also have conflicts and soul searching related to specific issues of childhood, like biting or toilet training or the teaching of values, as we discussed in Part Three. These all come with the territory. But there are also common problems that you can avoid—difficulties that seem to relate to child care but in fact relate more to your own doubts and fears.

HOW PARENTS EXPRESS THEIR FEARS

Parents express their fear of being supplanted in highly individual ways. Sometimes knee-jerk guilt becomes knee-jerk blame. While one parent will blame everything that goes wrong on the fact that she's working, another feeling the same pressure may blame it on some aspect of child care. Nannies, sitters, and center directors all feel that the parents who complain frequently about cost are in this category—they are almost always as able to afford their particular kind of care as the other parents, but the cost has become a convenient label for their general feelings of dissatisfaction. If parents want to be critical, there is no end to possible complaints. If a sitter were more accommodating when parents had to be late, if the other kids in the center were nicer, if the day-care mother did more interesting things with the kids, if there were a softer mattress on the changing table. . . .

Some parents make unreasonably rigid requests of the sitter or teacher. They insist that their child be fed on a rigid schedule, or not held, or do without a pacifier or favorite blanket. Often, these parents are trying to be certain that their parenting rules extend into the child's day even when they aren't around and to prevent a relaxed one-on-one relationship with the teacher. Usually this stern attitude is a temporary one. As parents become more comfortable with their caregiver and realize that their child still needs them, they begin to relax.

Picky and rigid parents are not as common as those that one center director described as "noncustodial parents." It's a term from the language of divorce that custodial parents know all too well. The custodial parent is the one in the trenches—the one who has to be there for illnesses, saying no, bad report cards, saying no, drilling on brushing his teeth, saying no. The noncustodial parent seems to pick the child up from time to time and fill the hours with nonstop ice-cream cones and baseball games.

Now in all fairness, it's hard to find an ideal activity for a Saturday afternoon outing week after week. Parents feel compelled to entertain their child, and it's hard to be "on" every week. Indulgence is one obvious solution.

Many parents with children in child care feel the same pressure and verge on the same weekend indulgence, say people in the field. Routines for toilet training or naps or snacks are frequently abandoned on Saturday and Sunday, along with any standards for table manners or sharing or listening without interrupting. The result is what people in child care call "Monday morning behavior." On Monday mornings, many children are wild and noisy and unresponsive to teachers or sitters or routines; by the afternoon they are back into the swing again.

Some parents who pamper their children on the weekends may be trying to hold onto a son's or daughter's childhood. Children grow up more quickly when they are in any kind of group care—having other children to imitate means that they may be younger when they try some things (like drinking from a cup) and drop others (like baby talk). But sometimes the baby talk disappears at the sitter's and reappears when the parents pick him up at night. Parents who see their child's childhood speeding by may try to cling to pieces of it without realizing it by encouraging baby behaviors; children respond with the behavior they sense is wanted.

Then there are Super-Parents. They feel the pressure to cram a week's worth of high-class parenting into the hours before bedtime, plus Saturday and Sunday; there's the added pressure of knowing that even those few hours have to be shared with trips to the dry cleaner, the hardware store, and the supermarket. As one mother said, "You feel that every moment should count." There is a relentless round of trips to zoos and museums and library story hours. The attitude seems to be that if you don't program every minute, you will fall even further behind as a parent, even if you have no time left over for your own relaxation and pleasure. When parents do this, though, they put a heavy responsibility on the child to respond. The message is that they must appreciate my parenting or else!

Can you break away from these punishing routines? Yes.

But you won't change by arguing yourself out of your doubts. Instead, we're going to describe how to reassure yourself about how your child spends his days and then suggest a new approach to evenings and weekends. Just give it a try. Once you've had a few relaxed weeks, you'll find that (always excepting bad days) you've put the old doubts behind you without even watching them go.

HOW YOUR CHILD FEELS ABOUT CHILD CARE

In order to relax, you need to feel happy about how your child spends his days. Studies show that parents' chief concerns with child care are that it be safe and clean. Well, of course. But beyond obviously necessary health requirements, these concerns reflect the image most parents have of child care—as a place to park their children for the hours they must be away.

The underside of that "parking" image is that most parents also believe their child's day really doesn't begin till they pick him up at night. That is what puts unbearable pressure on parents to be rigid or to spoil or to parent their child relentlessly every waking hour they spend together.

How do you get rid of the pressure? In Chapter 6, we talked about how a child's time in quality care is spent. We urge you to spend a few mornings dropping in on your child's sitter or center to see firsthand what we mean. In good care, your child is on the go, making friends, and imitating other children all day long. His day can be as challenging, rewarding, and exhausting as your own. And—this is what will make all the difference in *your* life—at the end of his day and at the end of his week, your child needs the same kind of time off as you do. He doesn't need a regimen of rules. He doesn't need to be force-fed indulgences or broadening experiences. He needs to unwind. He probably needs to do not very much of anything, with people that he loves.

HOW TO UNWIND—TOGETHER

Since your child feels pretty much the way you do, for all your sakes, you need to leave the routine of the workday and the child care day behind.

This approach begins when you pick up your child. Most parents think of their child as counting the minutes till he's rescued. But if you realize that he is satisfied with his day, you can see too that he may in fact feel you are intruding when you walk in—he's in *his* space, talking with *his* friends, doing *his* thing. If you walk in tapping your toes with impatience, by doing so you tell your child as loudly as if you shouted that what he has been doing all day has little importance in your eyes.

Instead, try to plan a minimum of ten to fifteen minutes at pickup time. Sit down on what one mother called "that itty-bitty chair," hug your child, and talk to the caregiver. If he has built a sandcastle he wants to show you, admire its every detail—he may have spent the last hour protecting it for you from marauding three-year-olds, no small feat. It takes time to change the scenery in a play, and in a way that's what you are doing. If you become part of his group, when the two of you leave together, it feels natural to all concerned. If you bustle in and hustle him out, it's a harsh, uncomfortable break.

And once you are home?

This too takes rethinking. Whether we think about it or not, most of us divide time off into chore, or "wasted," time and free, or "good," time. We spend our lives rushing through one to get to the other. But as far as children are concerned, that's an artificial division, one we must teach them. Washing windows, walking in front of you with his hands hiked up to the mower's handles to help you mow the lawn, shoveling snow, even painting, are not chores to a child if done with you. Collapsing on the sofa to watch a baseball game is not necessarily fun *unless* he does it with you. Zoos and museum tours may be valuable parenting projects in your eyes, but if that means you do them solemnly and your child gets no sense of relaxed camaraderie, he'll probably prefer the windows or the lawn.

And that's one part of the magic formula: Get away from the artificial division between chores and "good" family time. It is *all* family time.

Once you begin to think of all your time together as family time, no one part of the evening or weekend is forced to carry the weight of being a meaningful parenting experience. Without the pressure to rush through shopping to get to the "good" time, you can do chores—all of you together—at a pace that the parents can survive.

And that's another part of the formula—thinking about *your* needs too. How, ideally, would you use an evening to restore yourself for the next day's work, a weekend to restore yourself for the next week? Your child is a member of your family; he shares your genes. Chances are he shares some of your tastes and your pace—and your lives together in the years to come will be much richer if he develops them. If you like King Kong and Godzilla, so will he. If you like tearing walls down and rebuilding them two feet away, so will he. If you like time to yourself after spending the week with others, chances are he too will want staring-out-of-the-window time, time off even from you.

One unexpected benefit of doing what *you* enjoy is that parenting will seem much simpler. Discipline becomes easier. If you go to an event not because you want to but because you feel it's a worthy parenting project, it's hard to feel good about whatever method of discipline you use when your child begins to whine.

Your own feelings are in conflict. You envy his open display of an impatience you may share, you're annoyed that he dares to be bored by your sacrifice, he's disgracing you, you know that you are disciplining not according to what is wisest but to look like a good parent in front of others. If you are doing something you enjoy, on the other hand, you know exactly how you want him to behave and you have little ambivalence about seeing to it that he does. That matter-of-fact attitude always leads to the best results.

Another area we suggest that you take a fresh look at is mealtime. In Chapter 6, we explained why many children do most of their eating during their child care hours. That makes it possible to redefine the dinner hour in whatever way works best. Doing without a dinner hour is not an easy concept for many parents to accept, by the way. For one thing, everybody and everything from grandparents to family television shows tell you that meals are prime family time. For many parents, too, dinner becomes part of the conflict of proving they are still good parents: If he eats for me, I know I'm still doing my job.

Perhaps for you a long leisurely dinner is part of your secret daydream for relaxing. If so, by all means make it a special—unrushed—family ritual. But many parents have already had a big meal just as their children have, whether it was with co-workers or a business lunch. Getting dinner on the table takes time, energy, and thought that they just don't have in great supply at the end of a workday, especially for a meal nobody really needs. A snack of fruit and cheese that you all genuinely enjoy may serve you better.

The same philosophy should hold true on the weekend. An immense breakfast on Saturday morning may be your idea of family time; it could just as easily be having the whole family curl up on the bed with your hands in the cereal box while you watch reruns of "Sesame Street," or cinnamon toast and the Sunday crossword puzzle. It may mean spending Saturdays at the mall, alternating the shopping you must do with window-shopping, ending with the world's largest ice-cream sundae shared by all of you.

Families also increasingly feel the need for a break from both work and home. On Saturday morning they may check into a Holiday Inn thirty-five miles up the road for a family weekend, returning home Sunday afternoon. Some pursue church activities with other young families. The popularity of the Disney resorts and their imitators are soaring for weekend family recreation.

You will probably find that you have to alter your approach to some of your favorite activities to fit your child's needs. A trip to the Indy 500 may be too much to manage with a toddler in the midst of toilet training (how do you explain the lines at the portable toilets?). That year you may picnic on your living room floor in front of the television set, explaining that one day soon he'll actually be there in person. If an activity can't include a child, you may choose to curtail or postpone it a few years. One father said, for example, that he had temporarily given up golf (which would take four hours away from his family weekend), substituting tennis (an hour and a half).

DRAWING THE LINE BETWEEN CHILD CARE AND HOME

Parents differ too on how completely they break away from child care routines. If a child is in the midst of mastering a skill like eating solid food or toilet training, for example, some parents will simply avoid all-day outings that would make these activities hard to manage. Others will pack picnic hampers and stop at every service station on the turnpike. Still others will go back to bottles and diapers for the day, knowing that they may be setting their child back a step but feeling that the family's experience matters more and that they are doing what *they* can handle.

This can be confusing to a child. He'll say, "We're not allowed to do thus-and-so," quoting a center rule, not a family one. It can be hard for a child to learn two sets of rules, yet no caregiver and family will ever agree on everything. Are parents then to feel pressured to echo whatever the center does for their child's peace of mind?

As we've said, that varies from family to family, and the line you draw will be a personal one. But there are some guidelines. Never demean the caregiver's rules. Say, "We do things differently," or "Well, you're not at the center now," rather than "They don't know what they're talking about." You acknowledge the caregiver's right to have rules, in other words, but make it clear that it's okay to do things differently in different places. Each is a part of his world, but the terrain is not the same.

The second guideline is that it makes more sense for both you and your child to relax routines but not standards of behavior. Use your own life as a guide. You may eat at different times and play softball instead of sitting at a computer on the weekends, but you treat people the same way; your sense of honesty and your sense of humor are constants. In the same way, varying eating, toilet training, and napping routines for your child won't matter much either. But biting doesn't suddenly become acceptable on Saturday morning. Neither does hitting a smaller child or lying. You can relax any *routine; standards of behavior* should be an all-day, seven-day-a-week concern.

As Sunday afternoon winds down, it's time for all of you to prepare for reentry to the week. This means calmer activities, perhaps a talk about what each of you will be doing the next day, a return to your weekday bedtime ritual.

What we are suggesting throughout is that you think of evenings and weekends as *family* time, rather than *parent-child* time. Indulge the *family,* not just the *child.*

Time spent this way will help you relax—which in turn will lessen fears that you are too exhausted and impatient with your children. They will lower your stress level by helping you prune away activities you really don't enjoy.

Along with the pleasure comes something far more important: These good times reaffirm your sense of yourself as a parent. Instead of assuming the artificial authority of a teacher or a tour guide, you become the head of the family, introducing your child with the natural authority of your expertise both to the tasks that make a family tick and to the things you love. Since these also happen to be the things that make your family unique, you are also teaching your child what it means to be a member of your family. It is with a renewed sense of family and of self that you all then turn to face the week.

CHAPTER FIFTEEN

YOUR SUPPORTING CAST
. . . .

No family lives in a vacuum. If both parents are pleased with their jobs, everybody in the family loves the caregiver, and time spent as a family is rewarding, but if grandparents, co-workers, friends, and neighbors keep up a nonstop barrage of criticism, you will have to struggle to keep believing in the way you live. You need praise and support and understanding from the other people with whom you share your lives. If you haven't got it, you must find ways to get it, either from the people you know now or by forging new relationships.

In Chapter 13 we talked about the support you need from your company. Here, we're going to discuss the help you give each other, the special needs of the single parent, and relationships with family and friends.

HUSBANDS AND WIVES

The most important support is unquestionably that which husband and wife give each other. If you aren't on the same side cheering each other on, you're less likely to make it. And yet several things can get in the way.

One of them is the failure to recognize a responsibility toward this all-important relationship. It seems to be nurtured the least and expected to bear the most. Job stress, child care stress, frustration over the pace of our lives on the all-too-frequent days when they seem to be hurtling out of our control—too often we vent our frustrations on husbands and wives. Perhaps at a particular moment one's spouse seems to be the safest, least damaging place to put our feelings.

A very visible seesaw is the division of domestic tasks between men and women. Just as women have more than their share of work problems relating to child care, they seem to bear more of the burden at home too. Studies show that the number of hours spent on domestic chores doesn't go down much when women work, nor does the man's time increase much.

We're not convinced that these studies are fair to men. If the chores classically assigned to women (laundry, cooking, cleaning, and the like) are measured, no doubt change has been limited. But what about mowing lawns, shoveling snow, changing the oil in the car, and taking the car to be inspected, replacing the broken window in the dining room, painting the house? Our observation is that both men and women have their hands full.

If your personal division is too lopsided, though, it makes life much more difficult. Part of the problem may be that many women have trouble sharing domestic chores. It may be the criticism of parents shocked at their son or son-in-law running the vacuum cleaner, it may be inner uncertainty about working, it may simply be that women haven't taken the time to think through the schedule to see what kind of help they really need. Whatever the cause, the result is that women frequently ask husbands to help and then correct and criticize the results.

Women who are successful at sharing chores with their husbands have a different attitude. For example, they never redo a task their husbands have decided to take on. If he stuffs the clean laundry into drawers unfolded, if he puts meltable rubber spatulas in the dishwasher, if he regularly forgets to put out the garbage and ends up chasing the truck in the morning, she bites her tongue. "Once you give it up, you give it up," said one woman. Standards of perfection have to matter less than having the task off your hands.

Standards of perfection are different from basic rules, by the way. Rules are things like crystal breaks in the dishwasher and hollow-handled knives come unglued, red shorts will bleed onto white shirts in the washing machine. Rules should be explained either ahead of time or afterward, never when a task is under way (when they are indistinguishable from criticism). Walk through a job before he takes it over: Knives go on the right side of the plate; remember how you like those tight corners on the bed? here's how I make them; I generally wash the red clothes and the jeans together. (Or let him wash his own clothes till his skill level improves—*then* give him yours! You can't afford to let him ruin clothes you wear to work.) And after the explanation, say nothing more even if you have to leave the room. It's not yours anymore. Good, bad, indifferent, praise or blame, it's his.

When it comes to sharing child care responsibilities, much will depend on the kind of care you have. Studies show that men are unlikely to take much of an active role when a family has in-home care. You can see why. Since a sitter or nanny is most nearly a one-to-one replacement for the mother, not surprisingly the mother is almost completely in charge—of finding, supervising, judging the abilities of, and if necessary replacing the sitter.

With group care, though, whether at a sitter's or day-care

mother's or a child care center, fathers are more apt to become involved. They must! As the jobs of dropping off and picking up are added to an already-packed daily schedule, both parents must participate. One drops off, the other picks up, or mother takes one child, father takes the other. Or the best child care turns out to be nearer father's job than mother's. The parent who doesn't pick up may have to stop at the dry cleaner's in order to get there before the shop closes. And so on.

Less obvious than job sharing but potentially just as damaging, according to family therapists, is the underlying resentment that many men feel about their lives today.

Why should that surprise anyone? When a woman compares her life to her mother's, while it's true that she must admit to a lot of craziness her mother never had to cope with, she can point to personal achievements her mother never had.

For a man, though, the balance sheet comparing his life to his father's looks very different. Let's face it, the everyday, ordinary suburban man in the fifties—your father, your husband's father—had a life that now seems as alien and unattainable as anything on "Lifestyles of the Rich and Famous." Lots of jobs to be had, a standard of living that went up every year, most parental responsibilities the purview of the wife.

In contrast, today's father is learning how to prevent ring around the collar. Having to admit that two jobs are necessary simply to maintain the same standard of living from year to year —that he can't provide as well as his father did—can be a humiliating comedown to a man. On top of that is the day-to-day pace of the life of a two-job family.

Since it's not acceptable for a man today to say that he's disenchanted with his wife working, say the therapists, the resentment is apt to come out in sneaky and maddening ways. One man just happened to embark on a huge domestic project whenever his wife took a job; she would come home to find the kitchen cabinets ripped out or all the bushes torn out and piled up on the front lawn. Another man planned vacations like three-month walking tours through Europe—hard for his wife to turn down yet impossible to fit into her work schedule. Other men find fault with their wives' jobs— "Entry-level jobs," said one man scornfully. Still other men become enraged when some part of the domestic work suffers—if they come home to a messy house or a slap-dash meal. Many men behave this way while still paying lipservice to the idea of women working. The unspoken implication is that the average working woman is better organized than his wife.

Few couples can settle these issues by talking. Yet you both need the husband to like his life—you have too challenging a life-style to tackle unenthusiastically. The missing piece, we think, is a good look at what a man gains from a two-career life-style.

There's the advantage of two paychecks, of course. But there can be more to it than that. Men today are freer than ever before to work at jobs they care about. One man, a child psychiatrist, said his wife's job gave him the freedom to work in public service. Men can pursue careers like teaching that reward them intellectually or emotionally rather than financially, or they can content themselves with a less demanding level of job success.

Eventually, too, as men are forced to become more involved in their children's lives, they begin to see how lucky they are. A father today is a real parent and a real partner. He is more sensitive, more involved, and may even be happier. Center directors say that once fathers begin to participate, they're very enthusiastic. When parents are divorced and children live with their mothers, a growing number of the noncustodial fathers seem to take an active role —perhaps because it's a way of being part of a child's routine without interfering with the mother, perhaps he feels more like a parent when he's in charge. Increasingly, centers try to nurture fathers' participation. We see a growing number of events like father-daughter breakfasts (for which, said one director, "the interest is overwhelming").

And once he is deeply involved in his child's life, a father no longer questions his participation. Thus center directors say that when parents are choosing child care for the first time, the mother most often makes the choice, though the father may visit before the agreement is signed. If the couple must change caregivers for some reason, fathers have definite opinions the second time around.

Learning to balance chores and learning to see the advantages of your life-style will make life smoother. Beyond that, though, you must keep in touch with the life-giving fun between you.

It's not easy. Here's a scenario for an all-too-typical evening: One parent puts the child to bed while the other straightens the house and washes the dishes. It's probably nine o'clock, because children who nap at child care have later bedtimes. The child isn't too anxious to fall asleep, so the parent curls up with her to coax her to relax, perhaps reading a final story. Result? One parent falls asleep upstairs, and the other falls asleep while waiting and trying to watch the news.

How do you avoid this? You won't always be able to. In fact, one of our guidelines is, don't expect what you can't have. Leading a complicated and busy life takes its toll, and one of the places it does so is in the bedroom. This isn't the honeymoon phase, where your interest easily and naturally focuses on each other. Now you're going to have to plan for intimate time.

Instead of expecting world-class free time every night, plan for special occasions. If your children are small, a quiet dinner out—just the two of you—is usually not very successful. Parents of small children are so tired so much of the time that the unstructured conversation of dinner (plus a relaxing glass of wine) will find you falling asleep over dessert. Trust us: It does get better, and in retrospect this period will seem short. But in the meantime, while your children are small, rent a movie or go out for a movie or a play—even the local high school production. Play miniature golf. Anything that gives you something to react to and talk about besides work and children and who's going to stay home Monday for the dishwasher repairman. In between times, sharing that glass of wine while watching the news will get you through.

Almost as important as getting out and doing something together is the way you talk to your child about it. Take the same attitude as you do toward your job: Don't apologize. "This is important to Daddy and me, and we're really looking forward to it." A child in any kind of child care is accustomed to other adults, so you can add, and mean it, "You'll have a good time too."

When your child has been sick, getting out together is even more important. Not while he's ill, of course. But once he's recuperating, think about yourselves. When children are ill, they're rarely at their most charming. You're probably tired, and you probably have cabin fever. If you want to avoid lashing out at each other through sheer exhaustion, plan a few hours out of the house to restore your sanity and your sense of humor. You must tend to your relationship—no one else is going to.

FRIENDS:
His, Hers, Theirs

Friends are also of vital importance.

Men's friends tend to come from sports and work, neither of which is a hotbed of sharing and caring. They have more trouble finding supportive friends than women do.

Think about that for a moment. Any working mother meeting any other working mother knows immediately that they share a crazy-quilt life-style; only the degree of craziness is in question. Men aren't so lucky. Does a co-worker's wife work? At a job as demanding as *his* wife's? How much does he help? How safe is it to complain without being considered a wimp by somebody whose wife is at home doing it all? Where does he find other men who are doing the same thing?

In child care, that's where. In any kind of group care, a father has the chance to see other men doing the same thing as he is. Day in, day out. In the beginning, as he brushes by other men in the foyer or in the parking lot, there's the simple relief of knowing he's not alone. But as weeks and months pass, he may well begin to talk to the other fathers—to exchange horror stories and shortcuts. It's natural to talk about children here, just as it's natural to talk about athlete's foot in the locker room of the health club.

Ironically, just as men are discovering this kind of friendship, women seem to be losing the knack of it. Their problem isn't finding potential friends, but finding time to pursue them. Whether you call it being an earth mother or a martyr, women tend to give spouse, child, chores, and work their fair share, then accept whatever time and space is left as their own share. That means there's little time left over for luxuries like friends.

Even if you could pencil some meetings into your schedule, planned encounters are the opposite of what you need. The kind of friendships that would help are those built of a few minutes here, another few there—casual, unplanned encounters. The kind that used to be common when most women were at home: cups of coffee, doing one's mending together, sitting beside backyard wading pools. Trust was built up naturally over hundreds of tiny conversations, each unimportant but adding up to the kind of unquestioning bond we are too rushed to build anymore.

The ways women search for friends today would be funny if it weren't sad. Some women are wary of expanding work friendships; others feel, as one said, "You have little choice. Where else do you have the time to meet and talk to people except at work?" Health clubs are common. Family therapists have even reported women signing up for group counseling simply to meet the other women in the group.

We suggest that for you as much as for your husband, child care can be a good source of friends. Some women take vacation days to sit in the park with nonworking mothers. Take time in the evening to chat by your children's cubbies at the day-care mother's house or at the center. What are other four-year-old girls wearing or refusing to wear? Does she have any suggestions for Saturday night sitters? It's probably as close as you will be able to get today to the casual conversations and friendships our mothers had.

Aside from personal friends, parents today need to make friends with other couples—friends for both of you. These are the people with whom you share stories and worries about your children, about the toll of working, about where you are going as a couple and as a family. You go on Sunday afternoon picnics together and cover for one another in emergencies. You heal and nurture and have fun all at once. These friendships are priceless.

They are also the most difficult friendships to forge. For one thing, it's a more complex relationship, because more people must get along for it to succeed. And children complicate matters. If their ages are too disparate, their activities will pull you apart. If your parenting styles and goals are too different—something you may never suspect before the children arrive—a friendship between couples can't survive.

Geography may be against you too. In large urban areas, it can be more difficult to meet couples—and the ones you meet and like may be what single men used to label succinctly G.U. (Geographically Undesirable). No matter how much you enjoy one another's company, if you live an hour of heavy traffic apart, you won't meet often enough to be good friends. (One of the rarely stressed advantages of child care near your home is that any friends you make there will inevitably live near you.) On the other hand, geography sometimes works *for* you. As one woman in the Midwest pointed out, when people don't live near their families, although that often means loneliness, it also means that you share classic family times like holidays with people living the same life you are.

One good source for possible friends is the people with whom you took Lamaze classes. You know your children are the same age for a start, which means not only that there will be possible playmates for your kids but also that as couples you are coping with the same issues at the same time—your maternity leaves will probably end about the same time; you'll be looking for child care at the same time; you'll be learning to balance your new post-child schedules at the same time. You may even be able to share a babysitter, or one babysitter may have a friend who is looking for a job, or you may pass on recommendations for child care centers.

Because of the difficulty of making such friends and the demands of your own lives, you will never have many couple friends. Don't try. Settle for three of four other couples whose lives and attitudes mirror your own.

SINGLE PARENTS

Just like their married counterparts, single parents need other parents in the same position. As with two-parent families, this is probably easier to do through group child care. We don't recommend looking specifically for a center with large numbers of single parents—a center with that narrow an emphasis may be narrow in other ways as well. Nor is it necessary because you will find single parents any place you go; centers report as many as thirty percent of their families are headed by a single parent. (The exceptions are small centers with a religious orientation.) We'll caution you as we did two-parent families: Don't look for a long list of butterfly acquaintances. What you need, in both practical and emotional terms, is three or four close friends.

Being a single parent may also affect your choice of child care. It may not be possible to live with the fixed hours of a center. A sitter or a family day-care mother may be more relaxed about hours, making it less of a hassle for you to work late. She may even agree to sit in the evenings or over an occasional weekend—important if you travel or if, like the majority of single parents, you try to keep your social life private from your children. Depending on where you live, this choice may also be a little more affordable.

While you need the affirmation of a few people living as you do, don't confine all your friendships to single parents. That may be an unnecessary warning—we find that singles are not very likely to single themselves out, so to speak; it's the rest of the world that pins on that banner. Single parents see themselves as everybody else does, in a half dozen different roles, from mother or father to worker to church member to tennis player. Single parents are represented in every political, religious, and economic group in the spectrum. Parent is only one role and being single only a part of that.

Nevertheless, if you need the reminder, here it is: Both you and your child need the community feeling of being with many kinds of families in many kinds of situations. If you are a woman raising a son or a man raising a daughter, your child needs to see role models of his or her own sex. When you isolate yourself, you tend to concentrate on the past, in which some things went wrong. Among lots of different people, you find yourself looking forward to what comes next. That makes it easier to hope, and hope has an energy we can all draw upon.

PARENTS AND PARENTS-IN-LAW

When you live close to your families, of course they are an important part of your weekends and holidays. In some cities and some parts of the country, children expect to live near their parents; in other places, that's the exception rather than the rule. That difference will in turn make a critical difference in your own lives.

We don't know if your own parents had a calm and seamless relationship with your grandparents, but we do know that this is a time of stress between you, the working generation, and the people your parents' age. We've mentioned some of the comparisons you are apt to make between your lives and theirs. What most people forget is that parents compare too. Mothers and/or mothers-in-law who stayed at home with their children often look askance at daughters and daughters-in-law who can't afford to do so or choose not to. To a mother, not making the same choice she did can seem like a criticism of her choice and thus her life. Then too, many mothers who stayed at home throughout their children's lives have since returned to work; they've had to settle for volunteer or low-level jobs that compare unfavorably to what their daughters or sons' wives are doing. Fathers who had little role in their sons' lives may, with grandchildren, begin to see and resent what they missed.

Ideally, parents would celebrate the positive changes in their children's lives. As of course they do—to their friends, to whom they brag about your achievements right along with the remarkable abilities of their grandchildren. But that's where the praise stays—outside the family. *You* are more likely to hear comments like "My son is doing the laundry?" and "I can't believe you're leaving that baby." When you spend a lot of your time tired and behind and having trouble believing it yourself, it's hard to respond coolly.

This can be particularly hard for single parents because they rely on their own parents more than couples do—in fact, many single parents move to be near their parents just because they discover they can't make it on their own. Many women who have lost touch with the fathers of their children nevertheless depend on their parents-in-law for help. Needing their parents and in-laws to make a go of it and for emotional support, single parents are under more pressure to find a peaceful way to handle differences.

Let's face it: You aren't going to change either set of parents very much. You aren't going to stop seeing them or to limit the time that you see them. And you know very well that the wisest thing to do in the long run is to ignore words that they don't mean hurtfully.

How then do you handle parents who are tactless? In two ways: One, be very clear to yourself and your spouse about what you choose to share with your parents. Don't look for emotional support you know you won't find. As one woman said, "You can't order Chinese take-out in an Italian restaurant." Don't talk about hot issues. If your parents don't like your working, don't tell them about problems with your job—thus you will avoid criticism that is both painful and hard to answer. If the concept of child care unnerves them, concentrate instead on how early their grand-daughter is talking. Confine your sharing to the good things—and, interestingly, to emergencies like family illnesses. They'll be delighted to help out; it allows them to turn comfortably back into parents again, reassured at how much you need them. And if part of the price you pay is an undercurrent of "See? I told you this life would be too much for you to handle," you'll be so grateful that you can overlook it.

The second thing you need to do is to lean on your friends. This is very important. Chances are they have to hear many of the same criticisms from their own parents. Talk about them. Scream about them. Your mother can't believe that anybody could take care of her delectable grandchild and not want to kidnap her? Your friend's mother wants her son to wear rubber gloves at the child care center to avoid infection. Once you know you're not alone—once you realize strains are an inevitable part of your age and your parents' instead of something painfully unique to your family—you'll find them much easier to shrug off.

Some of the people in your lives give you energy; some take it away. One guideline applies to every kind of successful support, from your spouse to friends to family: Try not to expect more than you will find. You won't have a whirlwind social life in these few years, nor will you have a honeymoon relationship, nor can you expect your parents to cheer you on. But if you look around with care, you can find a few rich and close friendships, a family that backs you up in some loving and important ways. And as for your husband or wife—well, when you reach out to each other in difficult times, those moments have their own kind of gold. Looking back, you won't want to trade them.

CHAPTER SIXTEEN

LIVING CHEERFULLY EVER AFTER
· ·

In this chapter, we want to take a closer look at the world in which you will live and raise your children—the world of working parents. There's no question that you have chosen—or had thrust upon you—a demanding life-style. But we want you to know about families—not just rich ones—who aren't merely keeping their heads above water but are living with energy and enthusiasm.

Similarities are important. They reassure you that you are not alone. Many—most—of the parents across the country with children the age of yours cope with the same problems that you do. We're going to point out the major things that successful caregivers and child care have in common, that all responsive parenting has in common, and that the lives of satisfied working parents have in common.

But differences are equally important. They help you to realize that you can put the pieces together in a way as individual as everything else about your family. Thus, once we've pointed out what successful child care and parenting has in common, we'll turn around and point out the significant differences we've seen in them.

WHAT GOOD CAREGIVERS HAVE IN COMMON

Let's begin with the things that good caregivers have in common. Whether they are sitters, day-care mothers or center directors, they *take their job seriously*. They value what they are doing. "This is the dessert in my feast of life," said one older worker happily. Good caregivers, whether they use the label or not, see themselves as nurturers. Not teachers (though they're often called that) who lecture and push children toward artificial firsts, like mastering a computer at the age of three. Not parking service attendants who merely keep children safe. Nurturers who allow and help children to flower in their own time and at their own pace.

Good caregivers *like children*. That sounds obvious, but it's not. You have to warm to children as separate, individual people to know that the toddler sitting in mouselike quiet underneath the crib is not miserable but sizing up the room and planning his next move, that the little girl who has chomped down on the arms of three fellows this morning deserves not a spanking and isolation but an ice cube to rub on her swollen gums, that the throaty gurglings of a five-month-old are first attempts at language that can be mimicked and turned into a game. She has the patience to wait through the two weeks of wall-to-wall bad temper that even the most appealing children can go through from time to time. She knows that loving children also includes keeping the bathroom clean, combing a child's hair, and keeping medical records up-to-date.

Good caregivers *are not using you or your children to fulfill needs of their own.* A good caregiver is not in this line of work because the only thing she thinks she can control is little children. She encourages them to grow even when that means growing beyond what she can provide—a day-care mother may even tell parents that their child needs to move on to a center. She doesn't *need* you in a disproportionate way. You're a part, but only a part, of her life, just as she is only a part of yours. You reach out to one another from positions of strength.

Good caregivers *respect parents and parents' needs.* They accept mothers who work and don't use it as a reason to criticize their parenting. They accept mothers who travel. Good caregivers understand that parents have less control over their lives than they would like to have—that the simple act of picking up a child on time may be the result of massive tactical maneuvering in the office, that parents are all too often tired and far behind schedule. They understand that working parents still want to share in the important steps in their child's life and that they are frequently uncertain about how to be a parent under these circumstances and guilty about real or imagined missteps.

A good caregiver also *has a game plan.* She has a clear idea of what a child should be learning at each age. Caregivers are alert to signs of language in babies a year old, to signs of readiness for sharing and group play in three-year-olds. But a good caregiver nurtures growth rather than just reacting to it. Whether planned by sitter, day-care mother, or center, activities will support and stretch the abilities of each age. The playground space for two-year-olds will be in peeking range of the three-year-olds to encourage imitation. Activities will change with the seasons and include holiday celebrations. Rainy days mean rainy-day activities rather than television.

A successful caregiver also *has a point of view.* She's not wishy-washy. Whether the concern is toilet training, the difference between truth and fantasy, or celebrating religious holidays, a good caregiver has given it thought and taken a stand. There won't be a permissive approach to discipline this week and a tough one next week. If the policy is not to reveal the name of children who bite, that policy holds in every single incident and at every level of authority.

A good caregiver *thinks a child's life is important*—and thus, that the job of providing child care is important. If child care takes place outside the home, the center or the space devoted to child care by a sitter or day-care mother is planned with the child in mind. That means safety and cleanliness, of course. But it's not only a matter of baby gates, weather-proof covers for the sandbox, and separate tables for changing diapers and eating snacks. Good child care space is decorated for the child, too. The paint is fresh and bright, floor coverings are clean enough to sprawl on, the most interesting things in the room are at a child's eye level rather than yours. There are cubbies for possessions, and they are low enough for the child to manage his own things. The space may even look disheveled and overstuffed to an adult, but if you hunker down to a child's level, you can see a fascinating world. (Conversely, what would look calm to you would bore a child.)

We're not saying that child care is easy or that there is enough good child care for everybody who needs it. What we are saying is that you don't need to reinvent the wheel. What you need to do is to insist that your caregivers meet the standards already reached by many people in all kinds of care throughout the country.

PARENTS WHO DO WELL WITH CHILD CARE

Just as important are the attitudes of parents who work well with child care. They share several qualities.

They *see child care as a process* rather than a decision made once and put out of their minds. Parents, child, and caregiver begin with care and feel their way toward a relationship that works for all of them. Occasionally, there's absolute agreement; more often, finding a common approach involves negotiation and cooperation. There are wonderful glowing days and downcast glowering ones. A child may outgrow a good caregiver, or a caregiver may move on to another stage of her own life. A child may spend days, even weeks, locking horns with a good caregiver simply *because* she's doing what needs to be done with him during a difficult stage.

But—and this is another quality all successful parents share—*the lines of communication always stay open.* When your picky daughter successfully tackles raw broccoli, you and your caregiver congratulate one another. When the gaily painted cores of toilet paper rolls are topped with popsicle sticks, turned into a squadron of helicopters, and suspended from the ceiling (posing traffic hazards to anyone over forty inches tall), you share a chuckle as you dodge them. When your son celebrates the birth of a baby sister by declaring war on the rest of his preschool class, you discuss ways of making him feel special and of helping him understand his tangled feelings. When the winter seems to be turning into one long sniffle, you talk about how to bring the germs under control.

Successful parents, like successful caregivers, *have a point of view.* They know how much they want to be involved in child care, and they look till they find the sitter or center prepared to match their own level of involvement.

Finally, successful parents *accept their responsibilities.* These change when your child is in child care, but they don't disappear. That means taking care of routine details like picking up on time, keeping your caregiver supplied with disposable diapers and baby food, and sending in money for field trips at stated times. It means not taking unfair advantage of a caregiver by things like requesting a sitter to do housekeeping chores when it isn't what you agreed upon. It means not taking child care for granted: keeping your caregiver informed when you need extra help—if you're working late or traveling—instead of expecting it automatically. It means knowing, accepting, and refusing to feel guilty about the fact that child care concerns may often need to be dealt with during your workday. It means reassessing your child care regularly, recognizing—with a minimum of self-flagellation—when one kind of care may not be working any longer and searching for the right replacement.

PARENTS AT PEACE WITH THEIR LIVES

Parents who are comfortable with their two-career life-style also have certain attitudes in common.

They are, first of all, *confident that child care is a real addition to their child's life.* Not all child care, not for all children at this point in time, perhaps. But they know that what they personally have provides excitement and enrichment for their child. That means the whole family can look forward without tension to the beginning of child care each morning, and there are no overtones of apology when they pick up their child at night. That means they respect and value what happens from morning till evening in their child's life rather than dismissing it as merely something that makes their careers possible.

Too often the topic of child care seems to hover under a big black cloud. People talk about the "child care problem," which sounds like a euphemism for trouble. Successful parents have a very different image of child care. To them, it has a lot in common with, say, a family vacation. Everybody accepts the fact that a family vacation takes lots of planning, lots of talk, lots of emotions, opinions of those around you, even quite heated disagreement. At some point, you have to pull out your checkbook. But nobody questions that the result will be a family adventure and a big plus in the family's life.

Successful parents are *confident that they are good parents.* To the too-common question "How can you leave that baby?" one confident woman reacted primarily with puzzlement. "He naps twice a day, so we have from five-thirty to nine every night plus every weekend. How much am I missing?" Successful parents feel very firmly in charge. They have few doubts that they can, through and with their caregiver, continue to raise their child according to their own standards and goals. Because they trust their own judgment, successful parents can listen to caregivers without feeling threatened, act on advice if it makes sense, and shrug it off if it doesn't.

Successful parents share an attitude toward work, namely: *Work matters—a lot—but family comes first.* Whether they have work that they love or work that they must do, they see it as something that allows their family necessary and pleasurable things it wouldn't otherwise have. Thus, a raise doesn't translate as power or money but as a family vacation or a new dishwasher. Work is kept in perspective. They won't bring work home on a regular basis; they are equally protective of the time they work late. They may turn down a transfer or promotion that would be bad for the family (or request one that would be better); they may negotiate with their boss for better hours; they may look for a new job with the same responsibilities but better benefits.

Successful parents *limit outside interests* for the same reason. They ration intrusions into evening family time. Volunteer work that involves a monthly meeting is possible, explained one father; a weekly meeting is too much. Much of the family's socializing is done with other families—even including birthday parties. Family time is family time.

Successful parents share some regrets too, by the way. They'd like to make a bigger contribution in their communities, they'd like a more active social life, they'd like more time for each other and for themselves. But what's more important is their attitude toward regrets. They *accept the fact that they can't have it all at the same time*—and perhaps they can have only a little bit of some things. Roast turkey and all the trimmings for Thanksgiving, for instance, but not a fancy dinner every Sunday. Brownies stirred up with the children for a special treat, but not a homemade dessert every night.

Perhaps these parents can accept the limits of their lives because many of them are a little older. They were single and childless longer, and they've put the high-powered social life behind them. And they see the present mix of work and family, too, as a stage. It's right for now, but it will change as the family changes. There will be glitches, too, from time to time, but they accept occasional crises and necessary changes as normal, not as a sign that there is something basically wrong with their lives. Their lives too are a process. As the children grow, there will be both more time and more reason to coach Little League or teach Sunday school. There will be time to have dinners alone and play tennis on Saturday morning, perhaps even time for that rarest of luxuries, doing nothing at all. Just as they feel on top of the present, successful parents *feel confident about their future.*

Now let's flip each of these—caregivers, child care, parenting, and life-style—and look at them from the other side: What are their differences? They're frequently just as revealing and helpful as similarities.

HOW GOOD CAREGIVERS CAN DIFFER

Good caregivers are not confined to a single category. They can be found across the spectrum—nannies, sitters, day-care mothers, center directors. Within each category, they can be from widely varying backgrounds; they can be found up and down the pay scale. They can be young, with a background of courses in early childhood and a commitment to this field for a career; they can be older, with the understanding and patience that comes from having raised their own children.

Caregivers may specialize. Some caregivers love infants, nuzzling, guiding first steps, treasuring fat baby laughs. Others are turned on by the headlong energy of two-year-olds or the electric curiosity of three-year-olds, or the first tentative reaches toward friendship and conscience of four-year-olds.

Good child care too comes in a hundred different packages. All centers will plan painting and outdoor play, but one may have painting projects daily, tie-dye T-shirts, and sprinkle glitter on glue, while three miles up the road, a center has a European emphasis on outdoor play—lots of it, twice a day in all weathers. Some may be heavy on Dr. Seuss books while others fill the shelves with Maurice Sendak. Some depend on their parents for help in the classrooms, while others discourage it.

The approach of good child care varies. One child expressed the difference to his mother in this way: "In the first place, when I cried, they told me it was all right to cry. In this one, they ask me where it hurts." The atmosphere in some homes and centers is full of hustle and bustle and noise; in others, it is quieter and more contemplative.

The goals caregivers set themselves, too, cover a wide range. Many of them reflect where they live—both the neighborhood and the part of the country. Some will teach their preschoolers the Pledge of Allegiance—and if they didn't, their parents would wonder why. Some emphasize manners. Some emphasize independence. They may have different beliefs and standards, which they will in turn pass on to the children in their care.

HOW GOOD PARENTS CAN DIFFER

Seeing oneself as a good parent also leaves lots of room for differences. Parents set different goals for their kids, from learning how to reason to making friends to learning how to catch and throw a ball. Some parents are firm about discipline, while others take it as it comes. In some couples, the fathers are frankly as interested in all aspects of child care as the mothers; in others, a man's interest is less obvious, confined to concerns for safety or learning skills. Some want an active role in planning programs; others are satisfied to choose a child care provider who shares their interests and goals.

Finally, the parents who are making this life-style work for them are as different as flowers in a garden. They have different incomes. That's obvious. There are other equally obvious demographics, like single, married, married for the second time with a blended family. Children come in all ages, with and without brothers and sisters.

There are other less apparent differences. Parents have different attitudes toward the role of their children in their lives. Some plan their lives around their children. They choose a house because of its child-oriented neighborhood; they watch to see what seems to interest their child, then plan activities to help that interest flourish. Other parents plan to incorporate their children into their present life-style. They pick a house they love, confident that their children will share that love. They count on their children sharing their interests.

Families have very different energy levels too. People tend to think that we all have equal amounts of energy unless it's sapped by guilt or poor nutrition or by doing something we don't care for. Unfortunately, that's not true. Guilt and unpleasant work are exhausting, but there's more to energy levels than that. Some parents adapt easily to the unexpected, for example, just as some children do, while for others, surprises are always unpleasant and draining. Some people happily allow half a dozen things to jostle for their attention while others prefer to deal with one thing at a time. Just as football players don't necessarily make good swimmers, parents and children have inborn energy quotients too. That means that some families will carry a physically demanding pace into the same evenings and weekends that others need to spend quietly unwinding.

Though successful parents all value family time, they have a hundred different ways to spend it. Growing numbers go to health clubs, where the children attend an aerobics class while their parents work out. Others go to neighborhood fairs and parades and waterfront art exhibits and flea markets. Still others may spend every Wednesday evening in church, where the kids will be in one corner playing while their parents are in another in a Bible study class. Shopping malls have mushroomed in popularity because they aren't just for shopping anymore; they are the setting for family events. The same thing is true of places like New York's South Street Seaport, Boston's Faneuil Hall, and Denver's Larimer Square. Some gambling casinos plan for the family too, running a circus for the children in the midst of slot machines for the parents. You can see young families in video stores on Saturday morning, stocking up for a house-bound weekend.

We treasure the differences in caregivers and child care and parenting and families. We think they are paradoxically the most important thing that all families in child care have in common, and that is the fact that each family can *choose* a kind of child care they're comfortable with.

You can choose. You need not settle for common-denominator child care whether planned by your neighbors or by people halfway across the country whose life is a hundred and eighty degrees away from your own. You need not settle for an approach or standards or tastes that make you uncomfortable. There is a wide enough range to please everybody.

Just as there is a wide enough variety among caregivers. Given time and effort, each of you, with your one-of-a-kind blend of needs and temperament and income, can find a caregiver—a good one—you like. Really like. Someone who fits your family and your life.

It takes thought and planning and energy, but, like that family vacation, you'll never regret the effort.

Bon voyage.

INDEX

· · · · · · · ·

Advertising for caregivers, 14, 55–56
Agencies, 67
  for family day care, 20, 56
  for live-in care, 14, 56
  resource and referral agencies, 56
  for temporary care, 119–20
Allergies, 45–46, 91
Au pairs, 11, 12–13, 14–15
  See also Live-in care

Babysitters, 10, 15
  advantages of, 15–16
  away-from-home situations, 123–24
  center teachers as, 80, 121
  costs of, 15
  disadvantages of, 16–17
  disagreements between parents and
    sitter, 99–103, 112–13

good sitters, characteristics of, 59–
    61, 239–41, 245–46
  interviews with, 61, 116
  outgrowing the sitter, 177–79
  rules of the job, development of,
    112–13
  salary issues, 113
  social-life concerns, 101–3
  as vanishing source of child care, 17
Babysitting services, 119
Background checks of caregivers, 61,
    116
Back-up care systems, 116
  combination care and, 36
  designated back-up person, 127
  for illnesses of caregivers, 28, 62
  for illnesses of children, 76, 81,
    187–88

"no advance warning" situations, 126–27
Banks, Ann, 167
Behavior management. *See* Redirection
Birthdays, 173–74
Biting
   caregivers' reactions to, 138–39
   changing child care because of, 180–81
   children's feelings about, 139
   onset of, 137
   parent–caregiver cooperation in dealing with, 139–40
   parents' reactions to, 138
   reasons for, 137–38
Bonding by parent and child, 47
Bosses' attitudes toward working parents, 207–8
Breakfast served at centers, 21, 90, 199
Bully/victim relationships, 158–59

California, school registration laws, 159–60
Car use by live-in caregivers, 103
Center-based child care, 20–21
   assessment of, 62–63, 64–65
   bathrooms, 64
   bully/victim relationships, 158–59
   as businesses, 23–24
   changing to a new center. *See* Changing child care
   directors of, 21, 81
   disagreements between parents and caregivers, 106–8, 114
   enrollment agreements, 74–75
   food and menus, 21, 90, 92, 199
   friendships among children, 156–58
   good caregivers, characteristics of, 59–61, 239–41, 245–46
   groupings of children, 21
   illness, policies on, 81–82
   infant care in, 10, 21, 64–65
   initiatives by children in play, 155–56
   national chains, 24
   parental involvement, 33–34
   parental visiting, 64
   parents' concerns about, 154–59
   personal time for children, 154–55
   personnel to talk with about problems, 80–81
   planned day, negative aspects of, 106–7
   policy-related problems, dealing with, 114
   regulation of. *See* Regulation, governmental
   services offered by, 10
   sex stereotyping in, 155
   teacher/child ratio, 62
   teachers as after-work babysitters, 80, 121
   types of, 22–25
Changing child care
   reasons to change, 176
   center's request that child be withdrawn, 188–89
   illnesses, recurrent, 185–88
   outgrowing group care, 179–80
   outgrowing in-home care, 177–79
   serious trouble with other children, 180–82
   sexual experimentation and abuse, 182–85
   tips on changing, 189–90
Chicken pox, 186
Child abuse, 183–85
Child–caregiver relationship, 84, 85–86, 213–14
Child's needs in child care, 41–42

anxiety related to new surroundings and, 47–49
health-related needs, 45–46
learning skills *v* play, 50–53
physical/emotional milestones and, 46–47
temperament and, 42–45
Choosing a child care setting, 54
assessment of various care options, 59–65
influences on parents' choice, 28–29
limiting factors
distance between home and work, 27–28
financial limitations, 34–36, 38–39
geographic location, 28–30
involvement in child care, degree of interest in, 32–34
job-related concerns, 30–32
in multi-child families, 37–39
for single parents, 39–40
making the decision, 67–68
parents' needs, consideration of, 65–67
sources for caregivers, 54–56
See also Interviews with caregivers
Church-sponsored nursery school, 22
Clothing for children, 77
College babysitting services, 15
Combination child care, 36
for multi-child families, 38
for older children, 177–78
Communication between parent and caregiver, 110–12, 242
Corporal punishment, 66, 108
Corporate child care. *See* On-site child care
Corporate policies on working parents, 204–9

Criticism of child, parent's reaction to, 111–12
Curious George Goes to the Hospital (book), 164

Day-care mothers. *See* Family day care
Death in a child's family, 167–68
Diarrhea, 186
Difficult children, 43
Dinner times, changes in, 92–93, 220
Discipline, 108
caregivers' approach to, 151–52
consistency between caregiver and home, 152–54
parents' attitudes toward, 150–51
repetitive behavior fostered by, 153
Divorce in families with children, 168–69
Domestic tasks, division between husband and wife, 225–26

Ear infections, 162–63, 186
Easy children, 43–44
Eating patterns, 89–93, 220
Elkind, David, 50
Emergencies. *See* Back-up care systems
Emotional problems, children with, 46
Employee Assistance Programs (EAP), 206, 207
Energy levels of families, 247
Enrollment agreements, 74–75
Evans, Nancy, 167

Family day care, 10, 11
activities provided by, 18
agencies for, 20, 56
ages of children in average group, 17–18, 104–5
assessment of, 63–64
bully/victim relationships, 158–59

changing to a new setting. *See*
Changing child care
costs of, 17
disadvantages of, 18–19
disagreements between parents and
caregivers, 104–6, 113–14
good caregivers, characteristics of,
59–61, 239–41, 245–46
interviews for, 61–62
off-the-books care, 19–20
operators of (day-care mothers), 19
parents' concerns about, 154–59
personal time for children, 154–55
policy-related problems, dealing
with, 113–14
sex stereotyping, 155
television-related problems, 104
toilet training and, 141
turnover in, 19
Family life and child care, separation
of, 221–23
Family time, 97, 244
children's need for, 217–18
tips for, 218–23, 247–48
Fantasies of children, 148
Fathers' involvement in child care,
226–27, 228–29, 230–31
Field trips, 75, 107
Financial assistance from employers,
206
Financial considerations in choosing
care, 34–36, 38–39
Finicky eaters, 90–91
Firstborns, 172–73
First days of child care, tips for
handling, 76–79
Flexibility in caregivers, 60
Flexible working hours (Flextime),
206–7
Food allergies, 91

Friends of children, 52
friends a parent dislikes, 157–58
making friends after moving, 166
making friends in child care, 156–58
neighborhood friends, 159–60
sitters and, 102
Friends of parents, 230–33, 236

Galinsky, Ellen, 197
Gender differences, parental
in domestic tasks, 225–26
in parenting, 198–99, 203
Gender stereotyping, 155
Geographical differences in child care,
28–30
Good-bye House (Banks and Evans),
167
Good caregivers, characteristics of, 59–
61, 239–41, 245–46
Grandparents, 234–36
Group care, parents' concerns about,
154–59
Guilt, parental
at home, 211–12
on the job, 196, 200, 201–2

Health problems, children with, 45–46
Hearing-impaired children, 46
Holidays, 174
"Hothousing," 50–53
Housekeepers, 10, 11–12, 14
See also Live-in care
Husbands and wives, support for each
other, 225–30, 237

Illness
back-up systems in case of, 28, 62,
76, 81, 187–88
of caregivers, 28, 62
center policies on, 81–82

in-home care for sick children, 124–26

parental absence from work due to child's illness, 203–4

parents' need for time together once child is well, 230

recurrent illness due to child care setting, 185–88

sick children brought to child care, 105, 107, 187

staying home, conditions requiring, 186

Infant care
center-based, 10, 21, 64–65

interviews with caregivers for, 59–60, 64–65

regulation of, 29–30

talking to child, importance of, 59–60

In-home care. See Live-in care

International Nanny Association, 10, 14

Interviews with caregivers
with babysitters, 61, 116

background checks, 61, 116

back-up systems, discussion of, 62

with center personnel, 62–63, 64–65

child-rearing issues, 66

duties and privileges, discussion of, 61

with family day–care mothers, 63–64

for infant care, 59–60, 64–65

with live-in caregivers, 61

observation at care center prior to, 59–61

parent-caregiver relationship, exploration of, 65–67

preparation for, 57–58

qualities to look for, 59–61

Intimate time for parents, 229–30

Jealousy, parental, 214

Jobs of parents
bosses' attitudes toward working parents, 207–8

changing jobs to meet family needs, 204–5

child care's effect on, 195–97

arriving late and leaving early, 198–200

company policies and, 204–9

coping with child care problems on the job, 200–2

guilt feelings on the job, 196, 200, 201–2

missing work, 202–4

studies on, 197

job and family concerns, balance of, 244

job satisfaction, impact on childcare decisions, 31–32

as limiting factor in choice of child care, 30–32

problems at home blamed on, 211–15

Junk food, 89

Lamaze classes as source of friends, 232–33

Language development, 148

Learning skills taught in child care, 50–53

Live-in care
car use by caregiver, 103

chores performed by caregiver, 11

costs of, 11

disagreements between parents and caregiver, 99–103, 112–13

family relationship with caregiver, 13–14
good caregivers, characteristics of, 59–61, 239–41, 245–46
hiring a caregiver, 14–15, 56, 61
interviews with caregivers, 61
for multi-child families, 39
outgrowing the caregiver, 177–79
parents' preference for, 13
rules of the job, development of, 112–13
salary issues, 113
social life of caregiver, 101–3
television-related problems, 99–101
types of, 11–13
Losing a child's love, parent's fears about, 213–17
Love felt by children, 213–14
Lunches, brown bag, 89–90

McClure, Jessica, 20
Madeleine (book), 164
Massachusetts, regulations in, 29–30
Masturbation, 182
Maternity leave, 47, 205
Measles, 186
Medical records of children, 75, 162
Medication-giving, 82
Meningitis, 187
Men's resentment about their lives, 227–28
Milestones in a child's life, 46–47
parents' wish to experience, 133–34
Miseducation, 50–53
Mom and Pop centers, 22–23
"Monday morning behavior," 216
Moving with children, 165–67
Multi-child families
combination child care, 38
costs of child care, 38–39

live-in care for, 39
same type of care for both children, 37–38
sibling relationships in, 38

Nannies, 9–10, 11, 12, 14
See also Live-in care
Nap periods, 93–94
Negotiations with children, 152
Neighborhood, importance of, 159–60
Neighborhood co-ops, 22
Noncustodial parents, 215–16
Nurturers, 239

Off-the-books care, 14, 15, 19–20, 30
Ohio, regulations in, 90
Once-in-a-while care, 115–16
full-time care for a brief period, 119–20
guidelines for, 116
"no advance warning" situations, 126–27
one-time care, 117
part-time care, 117–18
round-the-clock care, 120–22
for sick children, 124–26
travel situations, 122–24
One–time care, 117
Only children, 172–73
On-site child care, 1, 22, 24–25, 159, 206
Oral sex play, 182
Orthodontic correction, 164

Paperwork, 74–75
Parental involvement in child care, 32–34
Parent-caregiver relationship, 58, 145
communication, importance of, 110–12, 242

good relations, maintenance of, 79–85, 108–14
as interview topic, 65–67
live-in caregivers, 13–14
Parenting with the caregiver, 33
biting, dealing with, 137–40
discipline issues, 150–54
learning from experience of caregivers, 135–36
parent-caregiver relationship, importance of, 145
parents' picture of babyhood and, 134–36
special events, dealing with, 163–64, 165–70, 173–75
toilet training, 140–44
Parents at peace with their lives, characteristics of, 243–45, 246–48
Parents who work well with child care, characteristics of, 241–43, 246–48
Part-time care, 117–18
Part-time work schedules for parents, 207
Patience in caregivers, 60
Payments to caregivers
lateness in, 105–6, 108, 109–10, 188–89
promptness, importance of, 79–80
rules governing, 74
Permission slips, 75
Personality of a child, 42–45
Phone numbers for caregivers, 75–76
Physical drawbacks in caregivers, 60–61, 67
Physical problems, children with, 162–65
Picking up the child
adults authorized for, 76

family arrangements for, 198–200
lateness in, 105–6, 108, 109–10, 188–89
promptness, importance of, 79
time spent at center, 218
Pinkeye, 186
Planned day, negative aspects of, 106–7
Play, importance in childhood, 51–52
Play-oriented caregivers, 60
Play patterns, 94–97
Pledge of Allegiance, 174
Positive redirection. See Redirection

Quality time. See Family time

Redirection, 151–52, 157, 159
Regulation, governmental, 10–11
of cleanliness, 144
of infant care, 29–30
of medication giving, 82
of menus, 90
negative consequences of, 29–30
of rest periods, 93–94
of snacks from home, 173
Religious child care, 22, 34
Religious holidays, 174
Remarriage situations, 169–70
Resource and referral agencies (R&R), 56
Round-the-clock care, 120–22
Rule learning, 149

Self-control in children, 149–50
"Settling in" to child care, 78–79
Sex stereotyping, 155
Sexual experimentation and abuse, 182–85
Sharing by children, 149
Sibling relationships, 38, 170–71

Sick-child care specialists, 126
Sickness. *See* Illness
Single parents
　limitations in choosing child care,
　　39–40
　support systems for, 233–34, 235
Sitting services, 119–20, 126
Sleeping habits, 93–94
Sources for caregivers, 54–56
　See also Agencies
Spanking. *See* Corporal punishment
Stranger anxiety, 47, 48–49
Strep throat, 186
Super-Parents, 216–17
Surgery for a child, preparation for,
　163–64

"Talk-it-over" chairs, 152
Teasing, 165
Television-related problems, 99–101,
　104
Temperament of a child, 42–45
Temporary agencies, 120, 126
Temporary child care. *See* Once-in-a-
　while care
Time outs, 152
Toilet training, 60

accidents, dealing with, 144
caregivers' advantages in, 141–42
in child care settings, 140–42
child's readiness for, 142
imitation of other children, 140–41
parent-caregiver cooperation, 142–
　44
praise used in, 143–44
pressure on parents and child to
　succeed, 140
Traveling and child care, 122–24
Trust, learning to, 149–50, 155

Unions and child care, 1

Vacations, 122–24
Values, teaching of, 174–75, 179–80
Vomiting, 186

Weekends spent with children, 215–17,
　218–23
Wives and husbands, support for each
　other, 225–30, 237
Word-of-mouth information on
　caregivers, 54–55
Workplace, parents'. *See* Jobs of
　parents

About the Authors

ANN MUSCARI is vice president of corporate communications for Kinder-Care Learning Centers. For the last decade, she has helped pioneer the growth of child care centers that offer affordable quality care in a loving environment. Before joining Kinder-Care, Ms. Muscari served as director of the Lighthouse, a nonprofit youth counseling service; as a probation counselor; and as a social worker with the Youth Aid Division of the Montgomery Police Department. A member of the Child Care Action Campaign Board, she frequently lectures throughout the country on children and families.

WENDA WARDELL MORRONE is the author of *Pregnant While You Work*. Formerly a contributing editor and features editor at *Glamour*, she has written numerous magazine articles concerning women, families, and child care.